HANDCRAFTED PLAYGROUNDS

DESIGNS YOU CAN BUILD YOURSELF

HANDCRAFTED PLAYGROUNDS

DESIGNS YOU CAN BUILD YOURSELF

BY M. PAUL FRIEDBERG

VINTAGE BOOKS
A DIVISION OF
RANDOM HOUSE
NEW YORK

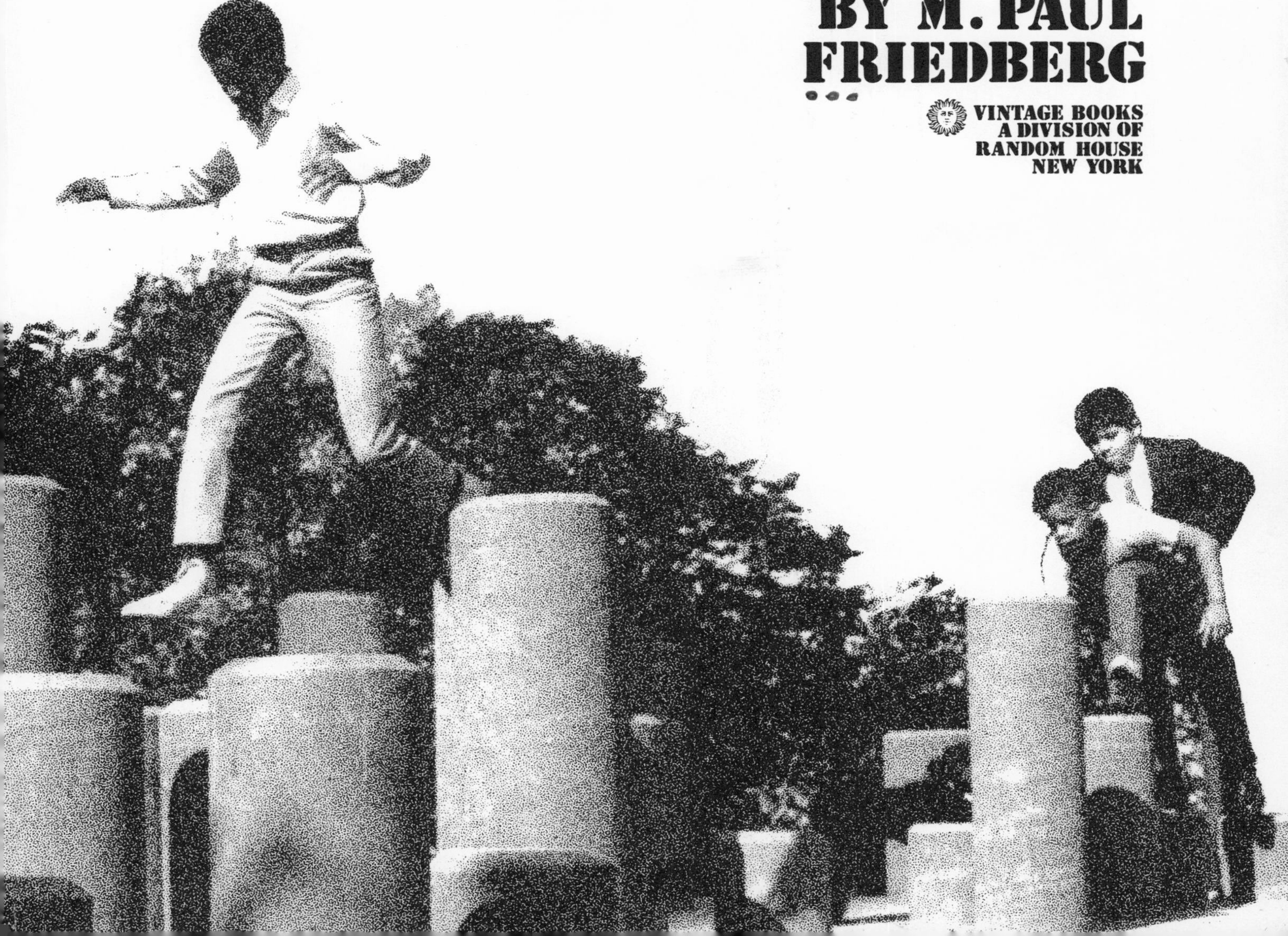

FIRST VINTAGE BOOKS EDITION   MARCH 1975

LIBRARY OF CONGRESS CATALOGING IN PUBLICATION DATA

FRIEDBERG, M. PAUL, 1931—
HANDCRAFTED PLAYGROUNDS.
1. PLAYGROUNDS. 2. PLAYGROUNDS-- APPARATUS AND EQUIPMENT. I. TITLE.
[GV424. F73 1975 b]   790'.068   74-22041
ISBN 0-394-71530-6

ACKNOWLEDGEMENTS

SPECIAL THANKS TO VINCENT TROCCHIA WITHOUT WHOSE ASSISTANCE
THIS BOOK WOULD NOT HAVE BEEN POSSIBLE.

ALSO TO TOM MOHR, BONNIE ROCHE, CYNTHIA RICE AND MY SONS,
MARK AND JEFF, WHO TAUGHT ME ALL I KNOW ABOUT PLAY.

ALL PHOTOGRAPHS BY M. PAUL FRIEDBERG EXCEPT PAGES
4, 64, 72, 84 & 123. THESE PHOTOS TAKEN BY RON GREEN
OF GRAPHICS 3, PORTLAND, OREGON.

TABLE OF CONTENTS

ABBREVIATIONS:

CONCRETE - CONC.
DIAMETER - DIA.

FOREWORD

HANDCRAFTED PLAYGROUNDS IS A SKETCHBOOK OF
DESIGNS BASED ON TWO VERY SIMPLE PREMISES: ANYONE
CAN BUILD A PLAYGROUND, AND THE ACTUAL PROCESS OF
BUILDING IT CAN BE AS IMPORTANT AS THE FINISHED
PRODUCT. IT GIVES THE BUILDERS (WHO SHOULD CERTAINLY
INCLUDE THE CHILDREN FOR WHOM IT IS PLANNED) A CHANCE
TO SHAPE THEIR ENVIRONMENT, TO CREATE SOMETHING
TO ANSWER THEIR SPECIFIC NEEDS.

I HAVE TRIED TO PROVIDE AS WIDE A RANGE OF DESIGNS
AS POSSIBLE, FROM THE SIMPLEST, LIKE THE TIRE SWING,
WHICH REQUIRES ONLY THE KNOT TYING OF ROPES OR
CABLES, TO FAIRLY COMPLEX WOOD STRUCTURES, WHICH
CALL FOR POWER TOOLS SUCH AS DRILLS, SABER SAWS, ETC.
AND I HAVE INCLUDED ENOUGH TECHNICAL INFORMATION
SO THAT THE SKETCHES CAN BE FOLLOWED LITERALLY
OR CAN SERVE AS POINTS OF DEPARTURE FOR THE
READER'S OWN SKILLS AND PREFERENCES. WHATEVER
YOUR EXPERTISE WITH TOOLS, THERE ARE PLAYGROUND
DESIGNS TO MATCH IT.

1

ALL SETTINGS, URBAN, SUBURBAN AND RURAL, ARE RICH IN NATURAL AND MAN-MADE MATERIALS SUITABLE FOR PLAY. EVERY CHILD, WHEREVER HE OR SHE LIVES AND WHATEVER SPACE IS AVAILABLE, CAN HAVE AN EXCITING PLAYGROUND. ALL IT TAKES IS A LITTLE IMAGINATION.

IN THIS BOOK I HAVE ARBITRARILY SELECTED MATERIALS THAT CAN BE EASILY FOUND OR INEXPENSIVELY PURCHASED, SUCH AS BARRELS, LADDERS, CANS, LUMBER, OLD TIRES, BOTH TO SHOW THE POTENTIALITIES INHERENT IN READILY AVAILABLE OBJECTS AND TO UNDERLINE THE POINT THAT BUILDING A PLAYGROUND NEED NOT TAKE A GREAT DEAL OF MONEY. BY REARRANGING, MODIFYING AND ADJUSTING THESE OBJECTS, YOU CAN CREATE ENDLESS OPPORTUNITIES FOR PLAY. FOR EXAMPLE, A CHILD IS DRAWN TO A LADDER BECAUSE IT SUGGESTS CLIMBING, WHICH IS FUN. BY PLACING THE LADDER IN DIFFERENT WAYS - UPRIGHT, SIDEWAYS OR OBLIQUELY - YOU EXPAND ITS POSSIBILITIES. THE MORE FLEXIBLE THE EQUIPMENT, THE MORE SUCCESSFUL THE PLAYGROUND WILL BE.

INTRODUCTION

KINDS OF PLAY

OUR NOTIONS ABOUT PLAY HAVE CHANGED MARKEDLY IN THE PAST HALF-CENTURY. UNTIL LATE IN THE INDUSTRIAL REVOLUTION, CHILDREN WERE REGARDED AS MEMBERS OF THE LABOR FORCE, TO BE PRESSED INTO SERVICE AS EARLY AS POSSIBLE. THE IDEA OF CHILDHOOD AS A PERIOD OF LIFE WITH ITS OWN INTRINSIC VALUE WAS SLOW TO DEVELOP. PLAY WAS SEEN AS A NECESSARY OUTLET FOR CHILDREN, BUT ALSO AS SOMETHING TO BE DONE AS FAR AWAY AS POSSIBLE FROM THE WELL-BEHAVED ADULT WORLD. THUS THE FIRST PLAYGROUNDS WERE FENCED-IN ASPHALT SLABS SPRINKLED WITH METAL FORMS.

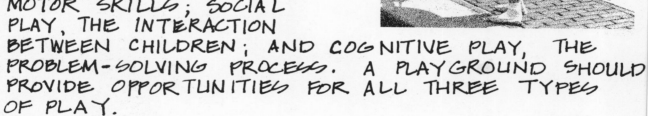

TODAY, HOWEVER, PSYCHOLOGISTS TELL US THAT PLAY IS AN INTEGRAL AND EXTREMELY COMPLEX PART OF A CHILD'S MENTAL, PHYSICAL AND SOCIAL GROWTH. IT CAN BE DIVIDED ROUGHLY INTO THREE MAJOR CATEGORIES: PHYSICAL PLAY, THE DEVELOPMENT OF MOTOR SKILLS; SOCIAL PLAY, THE INTERACTION BETWEEN CHILDREN; AND COGNITIVE PLAY, THE PROBLEM-SOLVING PROCESS. A PLAYGROUND SHOULD PROVIDE OPPORTUNITIES FOR ALL THREE TYPES OF PLAY.

PHYSICAL PLAY

<u>CHALLENGE AND TESTING</u>. CHILDREN ARE CONSTANTLY TESTING THEIR PHYSICAL POWERS, DISCOVERING THEIR LIMITATIONS, STRENGTHS AND PHYSICAL PROMISE. IF A PLAYGROUND DOES NOT PROVIDE SUFFICIENT CHALLENGE, THE CHILD WILL SEEK IT ELSEWHERE. THE CITY CHILD IS ALL TOO OFTEN FOUND IN THE MIDST OF THE EXCITEMENT ON A SIDEWALK OR A STREET

NEXT TO A PLAYGROUND, BECAUSE THE PLAYGROUND ITSELF IS NOT INTERESTING ENOUGH. IT IS ESSENTIAL THAT THE PLAY AREA PROVIDE EQUIPMENT THAT ALLOWS CHILDREN TO JUMP, SWING, SLIDE, CLIMB, CRAWL, RUN, FIND OUT HOW HIGH, FAR AND FAST THEY CAN GO. THE ADULT'S CAUTION TENDS TO REDUCE THE AMOUNT OF CHALLENGE BECAUSE ADULTS UNDER-ESTIMATE A CHILD'S DIS-CRETION. EVEN WHILE LEARNING THEIR CAPABILITIES, CHILDREN RARELY OVEREXTEND THEMSELVES.

AT THE SAME TIME IT IS ESSENTIAL TO TAKE INTO ACCOUNT A CHILD'S REACH, THE DISTANCE HE OR SHE CAN JUMP, CLIMB, AND SO ON, BECAUSE ALL ACTIVITIES MUST BE SCALED TO THE CHILD'S SIZE AND SKILL LEVEL. FOR EXAMPLE, A CHILD OF TWO OR THREE CAN STEP ONE FOOT HIGH AND JUMP TWO FEET. IF THE EQUIPMENT MEANT TO

CHALLENGE THREE-YEAR-OLDS REQUIRES STEPPING UP TWO FEET OR JUMPING THREE FEET, THEY ARE REALLY BEING CHALLENGED TO OVEREXTEND, FRIGHTEN, ENDANGER OR FRUSTRATE THEMSELVES. I ONCE SAW

4

A CLIMBING LADDER WITH PIPE RUNGS 3" IN DIAMETER, TOO THICK FOR A CHILD'S HAND TO GRASP FIRMLY. THUS A CHILD COULD NEVER FEEL FULLY CONFIDENT CLIMBING THIS LADDER.

MOST PLAY AREAS ARE INTENDED TO FUNCTION WELL FOR CHILDREN OF VARIOUS AGES WHO HAVE DIFFERENT LEVELS OF PHYSICAL DEVELOPMENT. THIS CALLS FOR A MULTIPLE SCALE, PROVIDING ALTERNATES. FOR EXAMPLE, WHEN DESIGNING STEPPING COLUMNS OR LADDERS, A VARIETY OF SIZES AND HEIGHTS SHOULD BE INCLUDED TO MEET DIVERSE ABILITIES.

SOCIAL PLAY

ROLE PLAYING. PLAY IS ALSO A TIME WHEN CHILDREN EXTEND THEMSELVES AND THEIR WORLD BEYOND THE LIMITS OF THEIR IMMEDIATE REALITY THROUGH ROLE PLAYING. A CHILD BECOMES A DOCTOR, A POLICEMAN,

 A COWBOY, AN INDIAN, A DANCER. BY SUCH ROLE PLAYING, CHILDREN FIND AND TEST THE PERSONALITY CONSTRUCTS WITH WHICH THEY ARE MOST COMFORTABLE AND CARRY THEM, AS WELL AS THE ABILITY TO WORK AND PLAY WITH OTHER CHILDREN, INTO THE REAL WORLD.

TO SUPPORT THIS SIGNIFICANT PART OF PLAY, IT'S IMPORTANT TO MAKE THE PLAYGROUND AN INFORMAL STAGE WHERE THE CHILD IS ENCOURAGED TO ACT OUT VARIOUS ROLES. AN ENVIRONMENT THAT DOES NOT LITERALLY PORTRAY ONE KIND OF ACTIVITY, THAT ENCOURAGES INTERPRETATION, STIMULATES THE CHILD'S IMAGINATION. IT CAN BE MORE "REAL" TO CONVERT A HORIZONTAL LOG INTO A PLANE IN ONE'S MIND THAN TO HAVE A READY-MADE TOY PLANE PROVIDED. AND THE NEXT DAY THE LOG CAN OBLIGINGLY BECOME A SHIP OR A CAR OR A HORSE.

INTERACTION. PLAY ALLOWS CHILDREN TO DISCOVER THEMSELVES, NOT ONLY IN RELATION TO THEIR PHYSICAL SURROUNDINGS BUT ALSO IN RELATION TO EACH OTHER. I'VE DEVELOPED A VARIETY OF DIFFERENT-SIZED SPACES, FROM AN INTIMATE, SMALL ENCLOSURE, WHICH HOLDS ONLY TWO OR THREE CHILDREN, TO A GOOD-SIZED TERRITORY, WHERE SHARING IS ENCOURAGED. THESE SPACES HAVE MANY DIFFERENT FORMS. SOME ARE TOTAL ENCLOSURES WITH A WOMB-LIKE QUALITY; SOME, PLATFORMS THREE OR FOUR FEET OFF THE GROUND, WHICH ACT AS A PERCH WITH SOME OF THE QUALITIES OF A TREE HOUSE.

COOPERATION. CHILDREN DO BECOME AWARE OF SITUATIONS IN WHICH IT'S NECESSARY NOT ONLY TO INTERACT SOCIALLY BUT TO WORK TOGETHER TO A COMMON END. THE TIRE SWING, WHICH ACCOMMODATES THREE OR FOUR CHILDREN, DEMANDS A CERTAIN GIVE-AND-TAKE, WHICH THE TRADITIONAL SWING DOES NOT. IF ONE CHILD TWISTS AND ANOTHER SWINGS, CONFLICT ARISES. IN ORDER TO MAKE THE SWING WORK, COOPERATION IS NECESSARY. SIMILARLY, PORTABLE PLAY EQUIPMENT TOO HEAVY FOR ONE CHILD REQUIRES A GROUP EFFORT TO BE USED SUCCESSFULLY, TO BE PUT IN PLACE.

6

COGNITIVE PLAY

PROBLEM-SOLVING. A WELL-PLANNED PLAYGROUND
PROVIDES A WIDE RANGE OF CHOICES, OFFERING A CHILD
MANY OPPORTUNITIES TO MAKE DECISIONS AND TEST
OUT THEIR CONSEQUENCES IN A CONTROLLED SITUATION. ALL
PROBLEM-SOLVING HAS A CLOSE RELATIONSHIP TO CHOICES,
TO DECISION-MAKING. IT IS MOST EASILY SEEN WHEN A
CHILD IS PROVIDED WITH SUFFICIENT ACCESSORIES OR
MATERIALS TO MAKE BASIC CHANGES IN THE PLAN OF THE
PLAYGROUND. THIS IS A CREATIVE ACTIVITY WHERE THE
CHILD IS SOLVING THE PROBLEMS OF PLACING LUMBER,
STUDYING THE INCLINES OF SLIDES, CREATING ENCLOSURES,
IN OTHER WORDS, ALTERING THE ENVIRONMENT TO PROVIDE

FOR A WIDER VARIETY OF EXPERIENCES. THEREFORE, THE
RICHER THE FABRIC OF THE PLAYGROUND, THE MORE
CHALLENGING THESE PROBLEMS WILL BE, AND THE MORE
INNOVATIVE THE SOLUTIONS MUST BE. GIVE A CHILD THE
CHOICE OF GOING OVER OR UNDER, AROUND OR THROUGH,
JUMPING OR PUTTING A BRIDGE ACROSS, AND YOU ARE GIVING
HIM DECISIONS TO BE MADE AND AN ENVIRONMENT TO
MANIPULATE.

7

OBSERVATIONAL LEARNING. BY BUILDING UP LEVELS INSTEAD OF LEAVING ALL ACTIVITIES ON ONE HORIZONTAL PLANE AS IN TRADITIONAL PLAYGROUNDS, YOU ALSO GIVE CHILDREN OBSERVATION POINTS FOR LEARNING BY EXAMPLE. PERCHES AND VANTAGE POINTS FOR MIXED AGE GROUPS ARE ESPECIALLY VALUABLE. IDEALLY THE DIFFERENT AGES AVOID PHYSICAL CONTACT, BUT INSTRUCT ONE ANOTHER VISUALLY.

GENERAL CONSIDERATIONS IN THE DESIGN OF PLAYGROUNDS

A PLAYGROUND IS A THREE-DIMENSIONAL SOLID. IT SHOULD ALLOW THE CHILD TO GO UP, OVER, ACROSS AND DOWN-THE RANGE OF EXPERIENCES THAT A CHILD ENJOYS. FOR INSTANCE, THE CHILD BEGINS AT GROUND LEVEL, CLIMBS UP A LADDER TO A TREEHOUSE, SWINGS ACROSS OPEN SPACE ON A TIRE, AND RETURNS TO GROUND LEVEL VIA A SLIDE. THIS IS INFINITELY MORE EXCITING AS A SEQUENCE OF ACTIVITIES THAN WALKING FROM ONE OBJECT OR EVENT TO ANOTHER.
NO MATTER HOW LIMITED THE AVAILABLE RESOURCES, THERE ARE CERTAIN WAYS OF LAYING OUT PLAYGROUNDS THAT PROVIDE A WIDE RANGE OF POSSIBILITIES:

LINKING. LITERALLY THIS MEANS CONNECTING THE ELEMENTS TOGETHER. YOU CAN LINK STEPPING COLUMNS, RAMPS, OVERLAPPING PLATFORMS, LADDERS. BY LINKING YOU PROVIDE PATHWAYS THAT OFFER FACINATING CHOICES AND INNUMERABLE OPTIONS. THROUGH LINKAGES, PLAY BECOMES CONTINUOUS. IF YOU CONCEIVE OF A PLAYGROUND AS A SINGLE ENVIRONMENT IN WHICH THE ACTIVITIES OF SWINGING, CLIMBING AND BOUNCING ARE EXPERIENCED AS THEY OCCUR AS ONE MOVES THROUGH THE ENVIRONMENT, AS OPPOSED TO SEPARATING CLIMBING FROM SLIDING, ETC., THEN THE PLAYGROUND BECOMES A SETTING FOR ADVENTURES.

8

JUXTAPOSITIONING. IN ADDITION TO LINKING, THERE IS THE JUXTAPOSITIONING OF PLAY ELEMENTS. PROPER JUXTAPOSITIONING AMPLIFIES AND REINFORCES THE ACTIVITY OF EACH FACILITY. FOR EXAMPLE, RUNNING DOWN A HILL DEVELOPS MOMENTUM. IF ANOTHER HILL IS JUXTAPOSED TO THE FIRST, YOU PROVIDE AN IRRESISTABLE FORCE WHICH CARRIES THE CHILD UP ONE SIDE AND DOWN THE OTHER, A RECIPROCAL, PENDULUM-LIKE ACTION. WITHOUT THE SECOND HILL, THE AMOUNT OF PLAY VALUE WOULD BE HALVED. (SPACING, OF COURSE, IS IMPORTANT: IF THE SECOND HILL IS TOO FAR AWAY THE MOMENTUM FROM THE FIRST IS LOST.) WHEN A CHILD SLIDES, HE SHOULD LAND AT THE BEGINING OF A PATH. MOREOVER, IF A PLAYGROUND HAS A HILL, BUILD A SLIDE INTO IT, MAKING THE CLIMB UP AND THE SLIDE DOWN A MORE ORGANIC RELATIONSHIP.

EACH FACILITY SHOULD BE MULTI-USE AND MULTI-PURPOSE. FOR EXAMPLE, MANY OF THE PLAY FACILITIES CAN BE USED AS LINKS AS WELL AS FOR SPECIFIC ACTIVITIES. A LADDER CAN LINK A MOUND TO A TREEHOUSE AND BE CONVERTED IN TURN INTO A SUPERSTRUCTURE FROM WHICH A SWING CAN BE HUNG. THE SUPERSTRUCTURE HAS AS MUCH PLAY VALUE AS THE SWING OR LADDER BY THEMSELVES. THE SAME STRUCTURE COULD BE DRAPED WITH CANVAS AND CONVERTED INTO AN ENCLOSURE. AN ELEVATED PLATFORM SO COVERED BECOMES A TREEHOUSE. TIMBERS OR LOGS CAN BE USED AS STEPPING LINKS OR FOR BALANCING OR STRADDLING. PLATFORMS CAN BE GROUPED TO CREATE AN INFORMAL THEATER. THE POSSIBILITIES HERE ARE TRULY BOUNDLESS.

THE EXCITEMENT AND USE OF A PLAYGROUND SHOULD LAST FOR YEARS, IF IT IS PLANNED FOR ADAPTABILITY AND

FLEXIBILITY. A CHILD EXHAUSTS THE LIMITS OF THE PLAYGROUND THAT CAN'T CHANGE WITH HIS CHANGING SKILLS, SIZE AND KNOWLEDGE. BEYOND THE PREDETERMINED ACCESSORIES. SUCH AS PLANKS, LADDERS, ADDITIONAL TIRES, THE PLAY-GROUND SHOULD READILY ACCEPT MATERIALS SUCH AS STYROFOAM, CARDBOARD, HOMOSOTE, ROPES AND STRING FOR MACRAMÉ, AND PAPER MACHÉ. YEARS OF INTEREST, STIMULATION AND ENJOYMENT CAN BE ADDED TO THE PLAYGROUND. MOREOVER, AS THE CHILD GROWS OLDER, THE ADDITION OF COMPONENTS THAT CHALLENGE INCREASED PHYSICAL SIZE AND STRENGTH AND ALLOW FOR CHANGES IN INTEREST IS ONE WAY TO ASSURE CONTINUED INTENSIVE USE OF THE PLAYGROUND. PLAYGROUNDS CAN BE CONSTANTLY REPLENISHED AND REINVIGORATED WITH IMAGINATION.

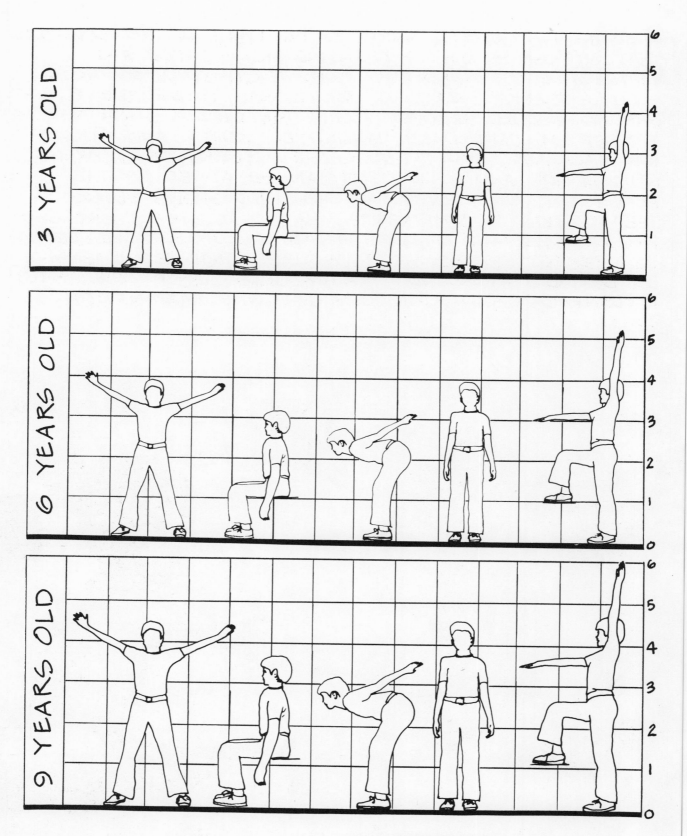

SCALE

ACTIVITIES MATRIX

○ PARTIAL
● TOTAL

	RINGS/HOOPS	SEE SAW	TIRE SWING	LADDERS	BRIDGES	RAMPS	SPRING PADS	CANVAS PANEL	WATER	TIRES	55 GAL. DRUMS	CLIMBER	SAND	ROLLER	BALANCE BEAM	NET	SLIDE	SLIDE POLE
PHYSICAL																		
CLIMBING				●		○				○	●	●				●		
SLIDING																	●	●
HANGING	●		○		○		○			○	○	●						
JUMPING						○	●		○	○	○	○	●			○		
SWINGING	○	●								●						○		
CRAWLING				●	○	○				●	●		○					
HIDING										○	○							
BALANCING		●	●	○			●			●	○			●	●			
SOCIAL																		
INTERACTION	○	●	●	○	○		●	●	●	○	○	○	○	○	●	●	○	
PARTICIPATION	○	●	●	○	○	○	●	○	●	●	○	●	○	○	●		○	○
ROLE PLAYING	○	○	○	○	○	○	○	○	●	●	●	○	●	○	○	●	○	●
COOPERATION		●	●		○	○	●		●	○	○			●			●	●
COGNITIVE																		
MANIPULATION	○	○	○					○	○	○			○	○	○			
PROBLEM SOLVING		○		●	○	○			●	●	●		●	○	○	○		
CHOOSING	○			○	○	○				○	○		○		○			
INTERPRETATION	●		○	○				○	●	●	●		●			●		
GENERAL																		
FLEXIBILITY	○		○	○					●	●	○		●			●		
LINKAGES	○			●	●	●	○	●	○	○		●	○	○		●	○	○
RESPONSIVENESS	○	●	●				●	○	●	○			●	○		○		

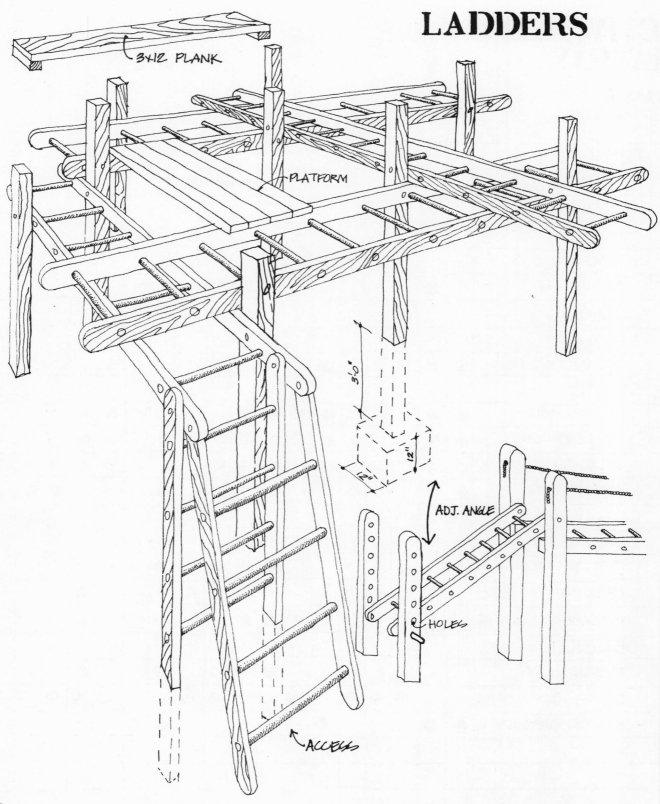

LADDERS

3×12 PLANK

PLATFORM

3'-0"

12"

12"

ADJ. ANGLE

HOLES

ACCESS

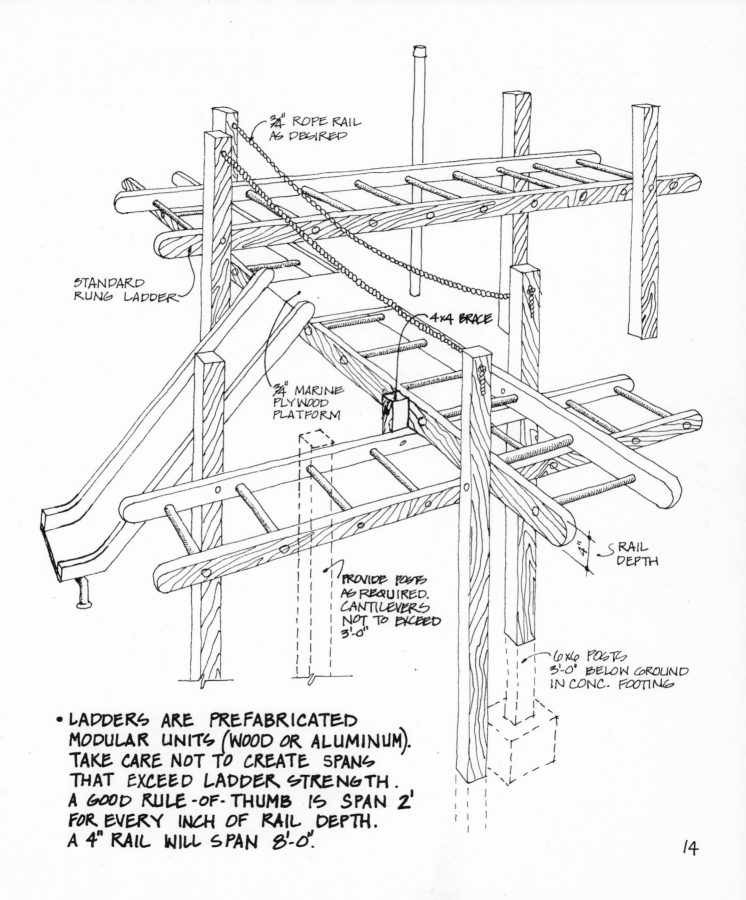

¾" ROPE RAIL AS DESIRED

STANDARD RUNG LADDER

4x4 BRACE

¾" MARINE PLYWOOD PLATFORM

4" RAIL DEPTH

PROVIDE POSTS AS REQUIRED. CANTILEVERS NOT TO EXCEED 3'-0"

6x6 POSTS 3'-0" BELOW GROUND IN CONC. FOOTING

• LADDERS ARE PREFABRICATED MODULAR UNITS (WOOD OR ALUMINUM). TAKE CARE NOT TO CREATE SPANS THAT EXCEED LADDER STRENGTH. A GOOD RULE-OF-THUMB IS SPAN 2' FOR EVERY INCH OF RAIL DEPTH. A 4" RAIL WILL SPAN 8'-0".

14

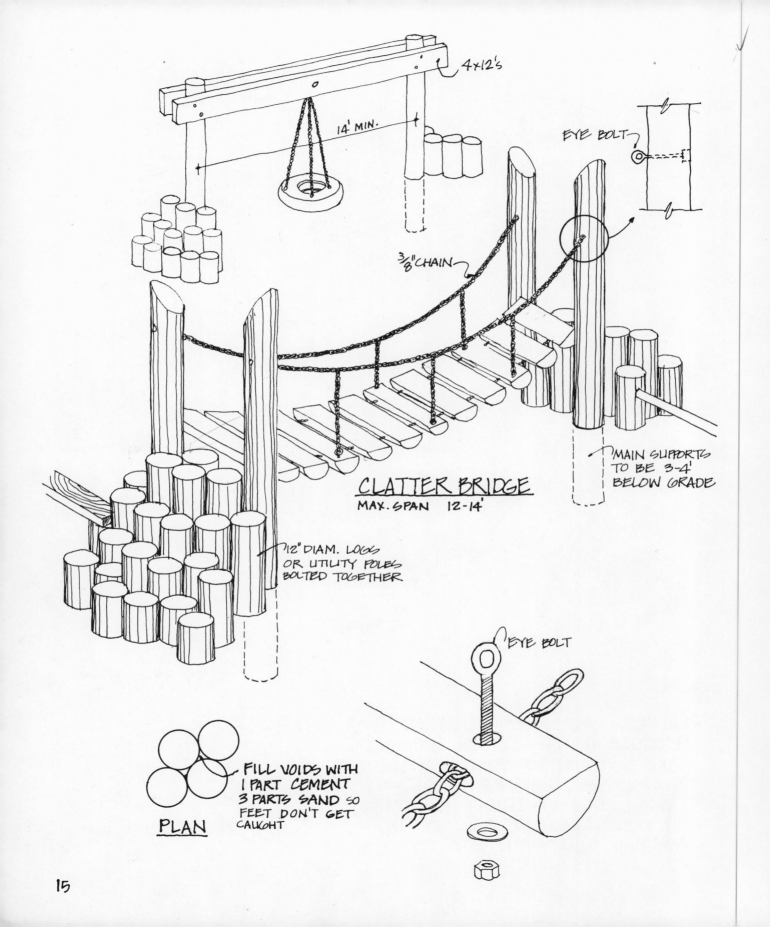

4×12's

14' MIN.

EYE BOLT

3/8" CHAIN

CLATTER BRIDGE
MAX. SPAN 12-14'

MAIN SUPPORTS
TO BE 3-4'
BELOW GRADE

12" DIAM. LOGS
OR UTILITY POLES
BOLTED TOGETHER

EYE BOLT

FILL VOIDS WITH
1 PART CEMENT
3 PARTS SAND SO
FEET DON'T GET
CAUGHT

PLAN

15

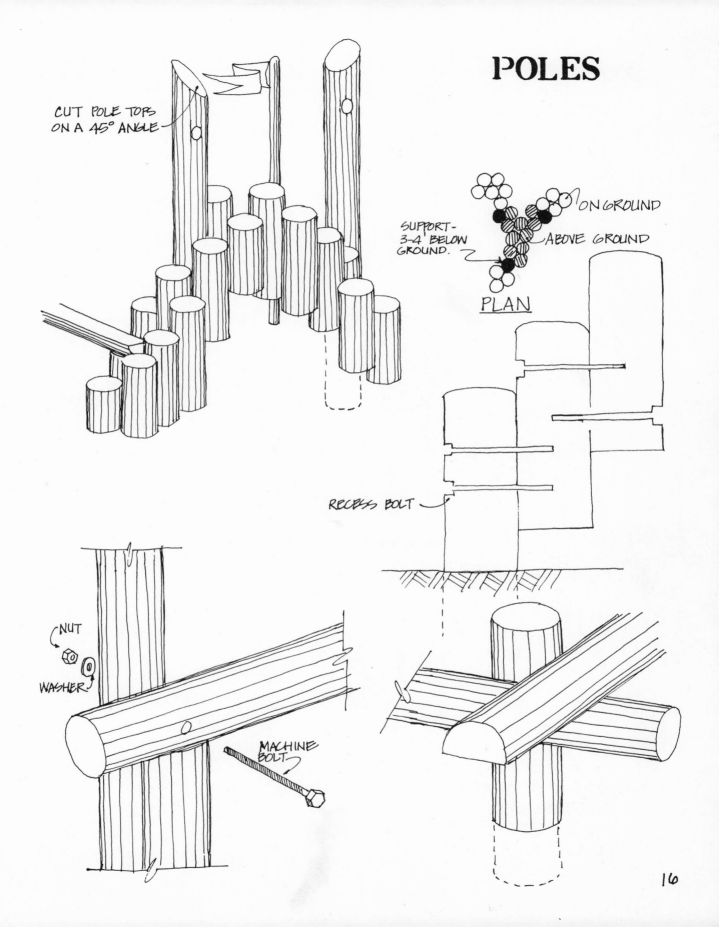

POLES

CUT POLE TOPS
ON A 45° ANGLE

SUPPORT-
3-4' BELOW
GROUND.

ON GROUND

ABOVE GROUND

PLAN

RECESS BOLT

NUT

WASHER

MACHINE
BOLT

16

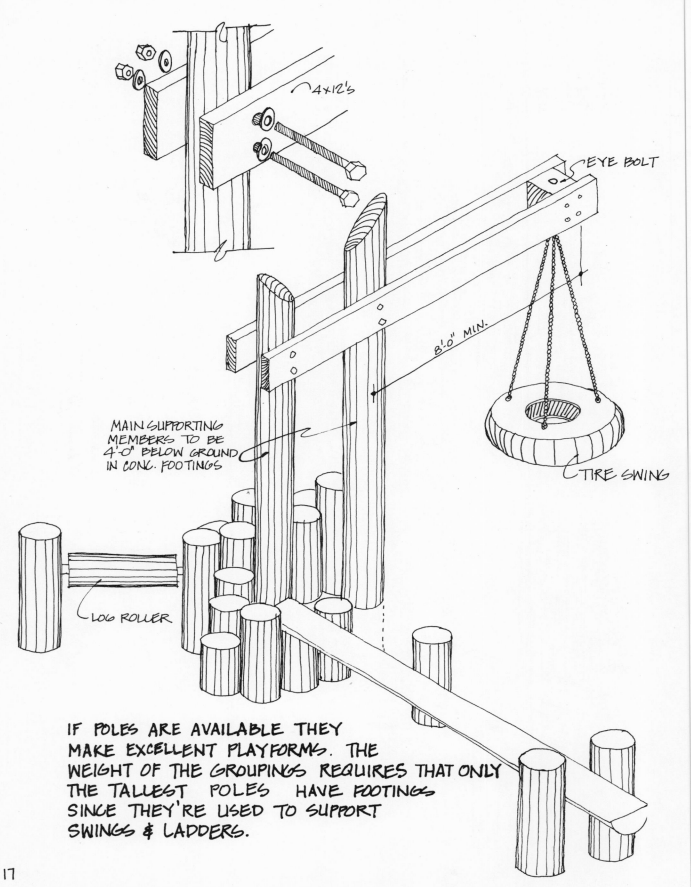

4x12's

EYE BOLT

8'-0" MIN.

MAIN SUPPORTING
MEMBERS TO BE
4'-0" BELOW GROUND
IN CONC. FOOTINGS

TIRE SWING

LOG ROLLER

IF POLES ARE AVAILABLE THEY
MAKE EXCELLENT PLAYFORMS. THE
WEIGHT OF THE GROUPINGS REQUIRES THAT ONLY
THE TALLEST POLES HAVE FOOTINGS
SINCE THEY'RE USED TO SUPPORT
SWINGS & LADDERS.

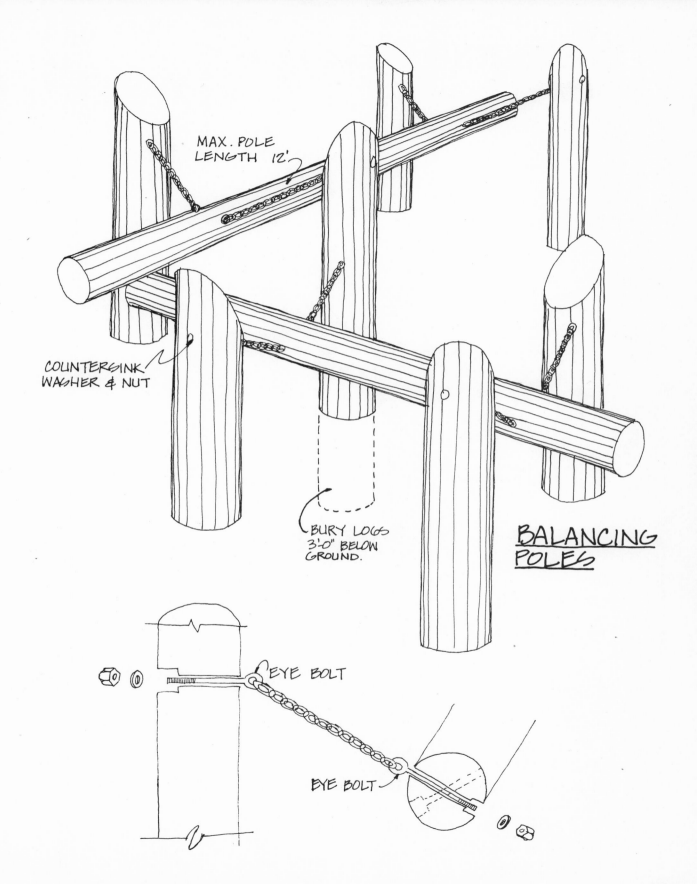

MAX. POLE
LENGTH 12'

COUNTERSINK
WASHER & NUT

BURY LOGS
3'-0" BELOW
GROUND.

BALANCING
POLES

EYE BOLT

EYE BOLT

18

POLES AND DOWELS

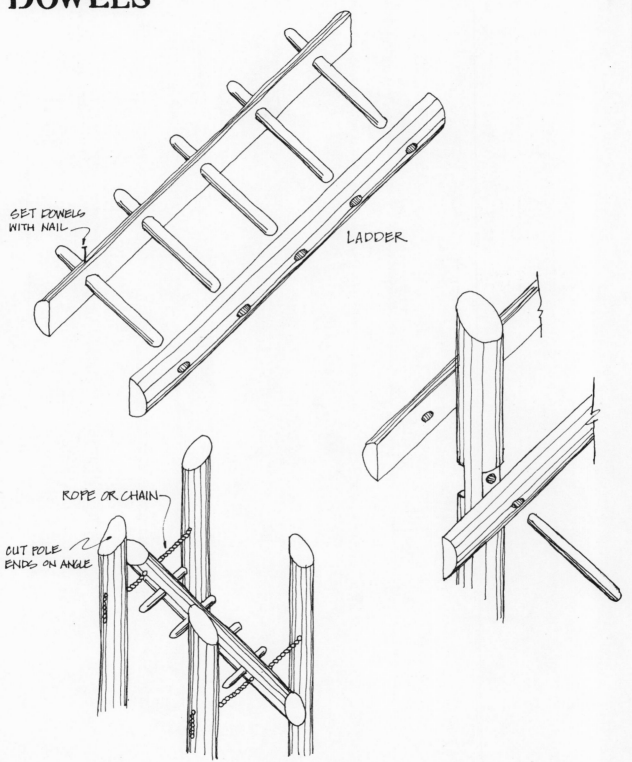

SET DOWELS
WITH NAIL

LADDER

ROPE OR CHAIN

CUT POLE
ENDS ON ANGLE

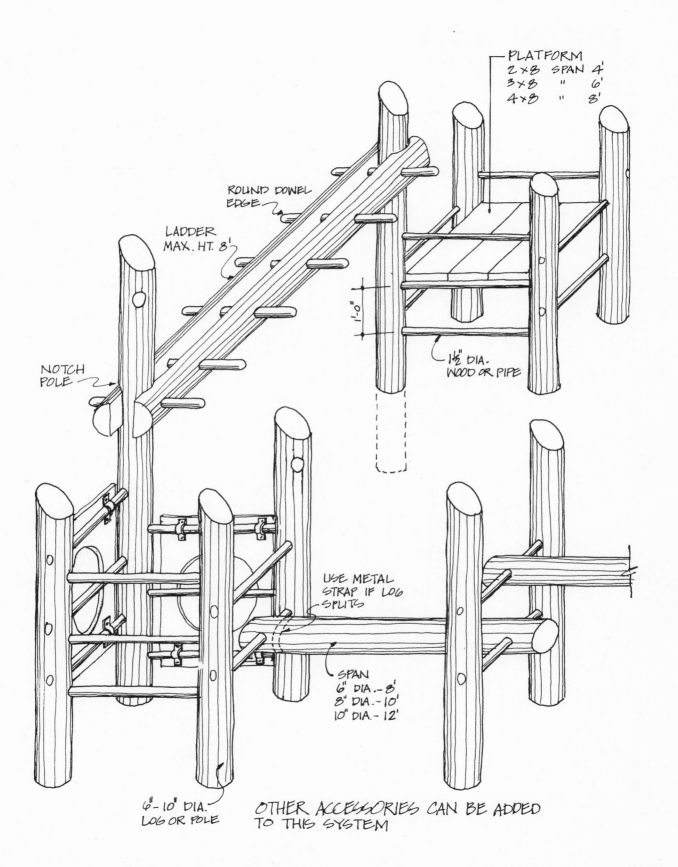

PLATFORM
2×8 SPAN 4'
3×8 " 6'
4×8 " 8'

ROUND DOWEL
EDGE

LADDER
MAX. HT. 8'

1'-0"

1½" DIA.
WOOD OR PIPE

NOTCH
POLE

USE METAL
STRAP IF LOG
SPLITS

SPAN
6" DIA.- 8'
8" DIA.- 10'
10" DIA.- 12'

6"-10" DIA.
LOG OR POLE

OTHER ACCESSORIES CAN BE ADDED
TO THIS SYSTEM

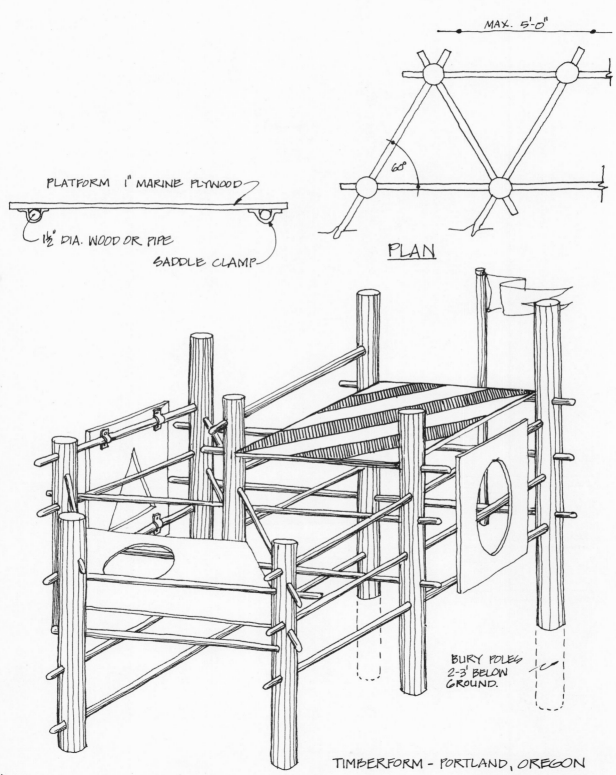

PLATFORM 1" MARINE PLYWOOD

1½" DIA. WOOD OR PIPE

SADDLE CLAMP

MAX. 5'-0"

60°

PLAN

BURY POLES
2-3' BELOW
GROUND.

TIMBERFORM - PORTLAND, OREGON

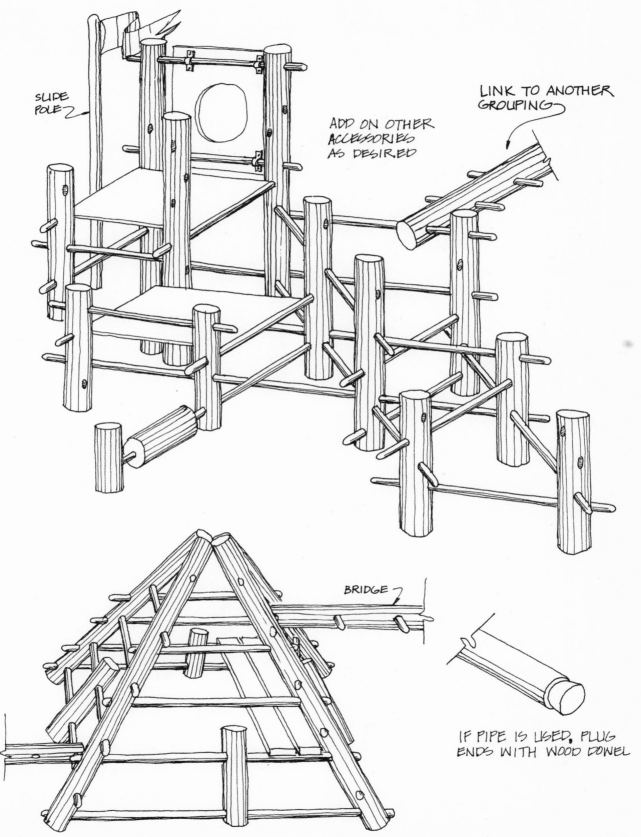

SLIDE
POLE

ADD ON OTHER
ACCESSORIES
AS DESIRED

LINK TO ANOTHER
GROUPING

BRIDGE

IF PIPE IS USED, PLUG
ENDS WITH WOOD DOWEL

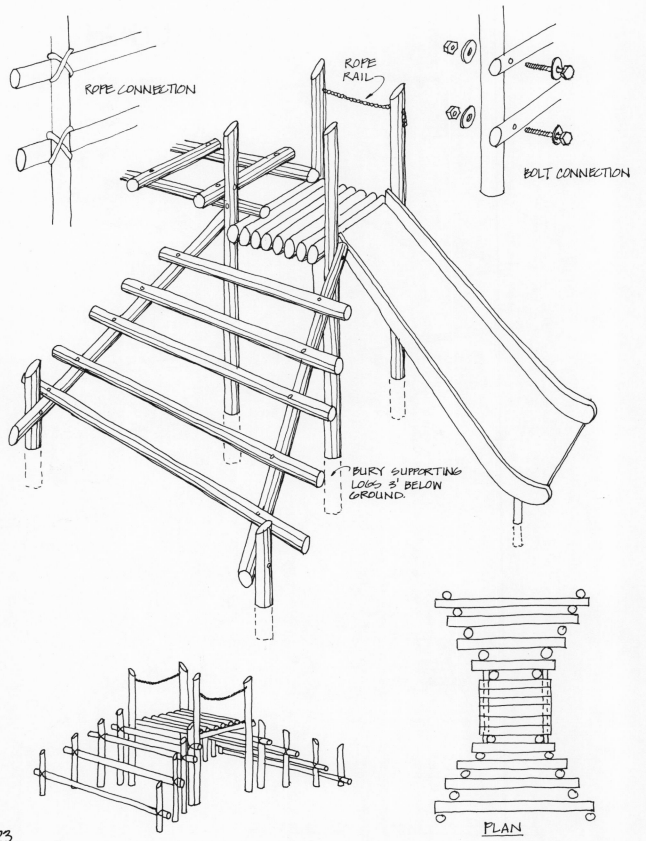

ROPE CONNECTION

ROPE RAIL

BOLT CONNECTION

BURY SUPPORTING LOGS 3' BELOW GROUND.

PLAN

LOGS

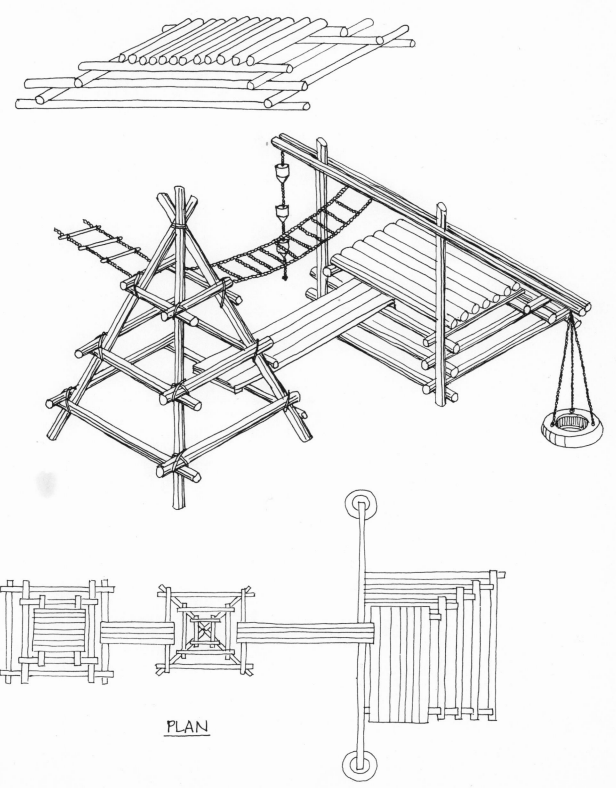

PLAN

24

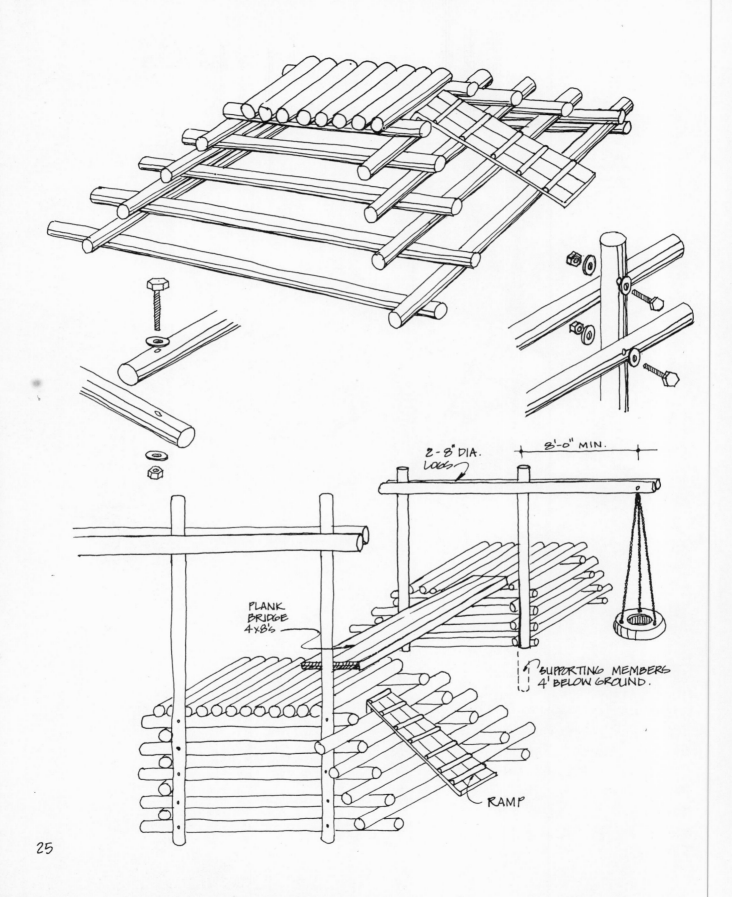

2-8" DIA.
LOGS

8'-0" MIN.

PLANK
BRIDGE
4x8's

SUPPORTING MEMBERS
4' BELOW GROUND.

RAMP

25

NOTES

FINISHES
EXCEPT FOR CEDAR OR
REDWOOD (WHICH HAVE
THEIR OWN PRESERVATIVE),
ALL WOOD USED OUTDOORS
SHOULD BE PRESSURE
TREATED, SOAKED
OR PAINTED WITH A
NON-TOXIC WOOD
PRESERVATIVE.
DO NOT USE
CREOSOTE AS A
PRESERVATIVE
BECAUSE IT CAN
BURN BOTH SKIN & EYE
TISSUE.

STEPPING COLUMNS

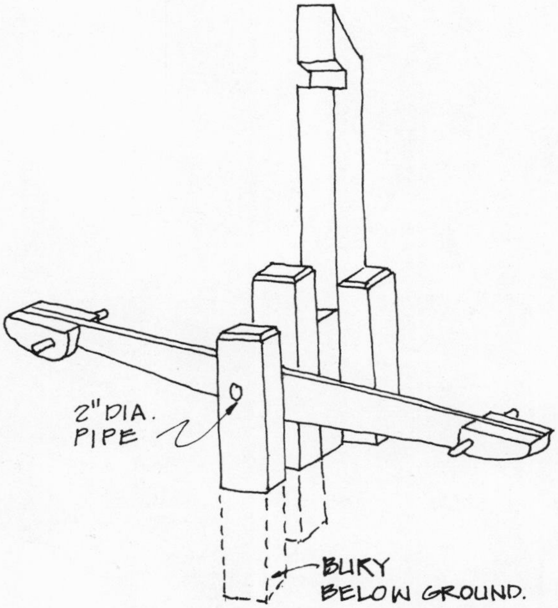

2" DIA. PIPE

BURY BELOW GROUND.

LAG BOLT PIECES TOGETHER

BURY 3'-0" BELOW GROUND.

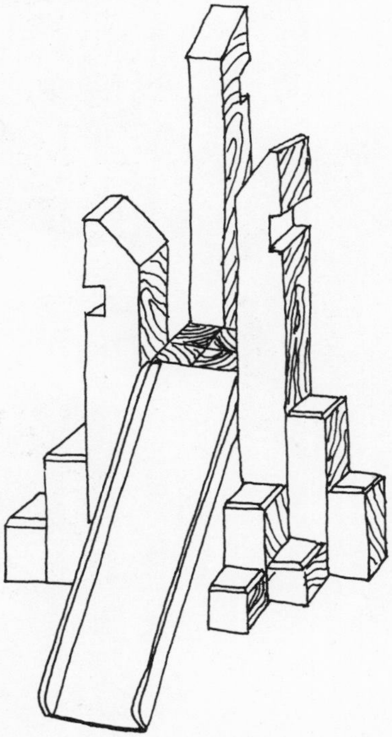

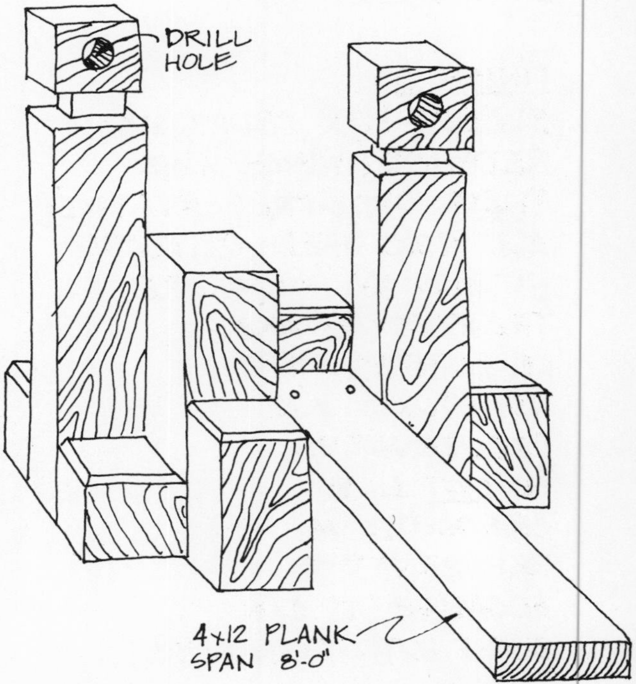

DRILL HOLE

4×12 PLANK SPAN 8'-0"

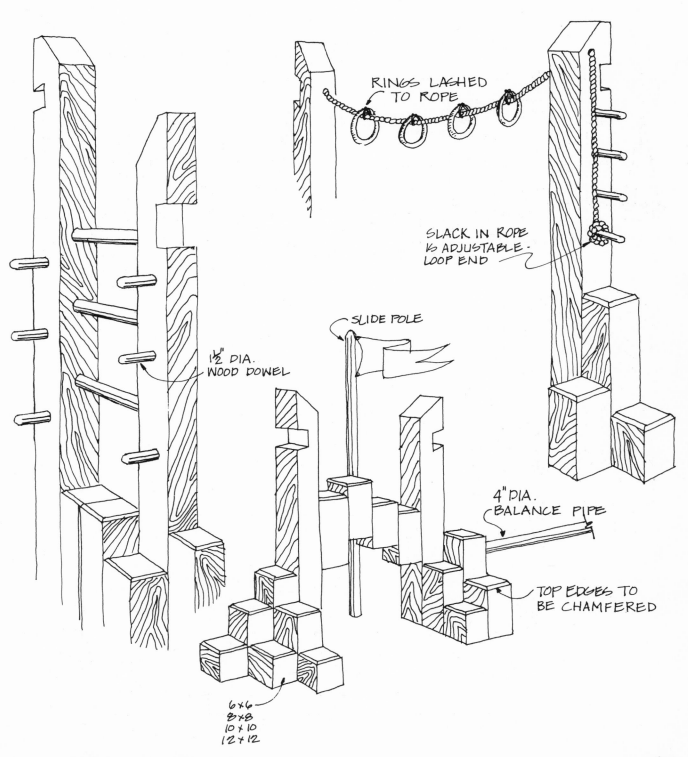

RINGS LASHED TO ROPE

SLACK IN ROPE IS ADJUSTABLE. LOOP END

SLIDE POLE

1½" DIA. WOOD DOWEL

4" DIA. BALANCE PIPE

TOP EDGES TO BE CHAMFERED

6×6
8×8
10×10
12×12

TIMBERFORM - PORTLAND, OREGON

28

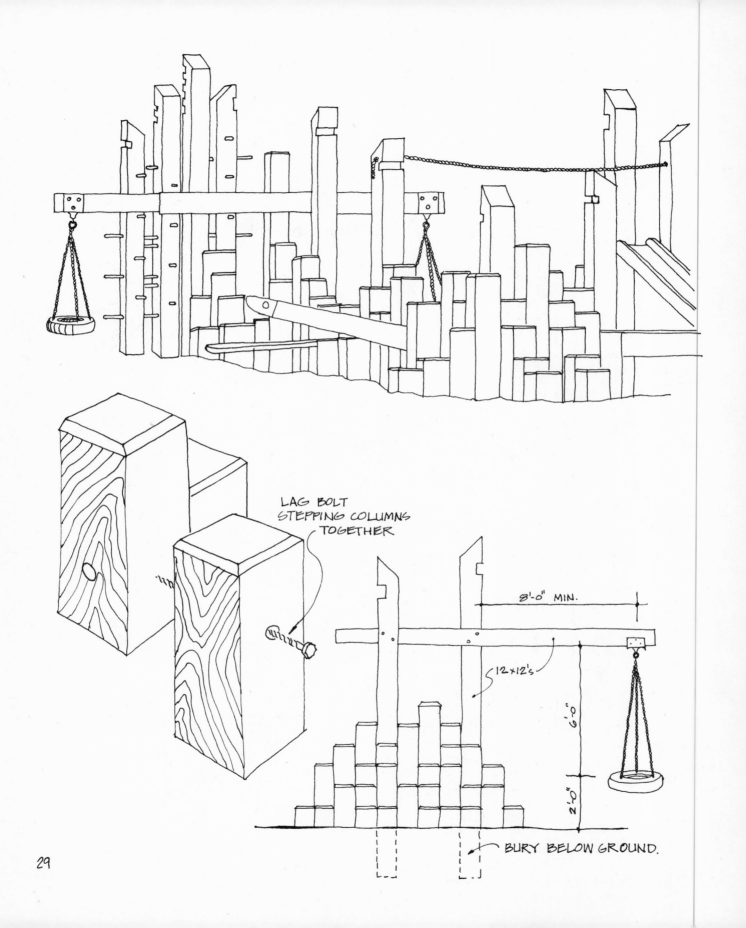

LAG BOLT
STEPPING COLUMNS
TOGETHER

8'-0" MIN.

12 x 12's

6'-0"

2'-0"

BURY BELOW GROUND.

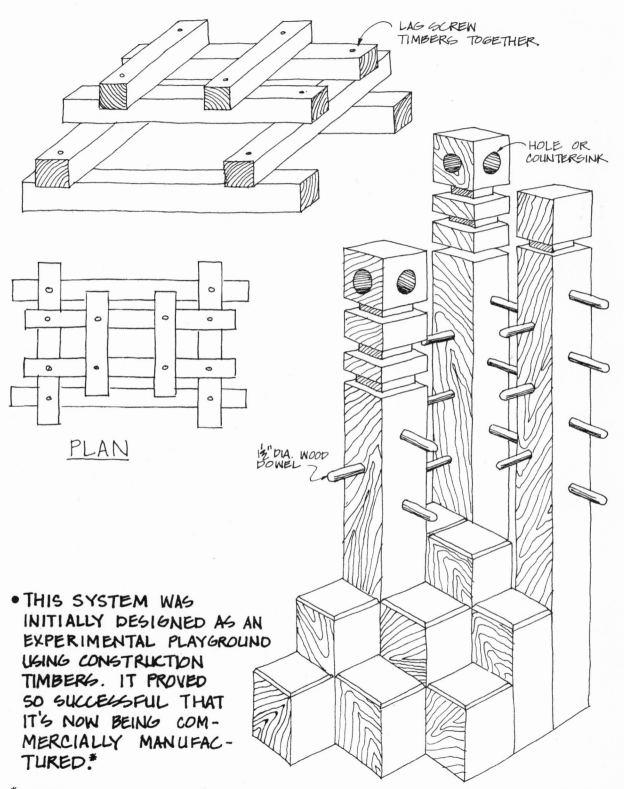

LAG SCREW TIMBERS TOGETHER.

HOLE OR COUNTERSINK

PLAN

1½" DIA. WOOD DOWEL

• THIS SYSTEM WAS INITIALLY DESIGNED AS AN EXPERIMENTAL PLAYGROUND USING CONSTRUCTION TIMBERS. IT PROVED SO SUCCESSFUL THAT IT'S NOW BEING COMMERCIALLY MANUFAC- TURED.*

* TIMBERFORM - PORTLAND, OREGON

POST AND CHAIN

THE POST & CHAIN
SYSTEM OFFERS
OPPORTUNITIES FOR
BALANCE AND
COORDINATION.

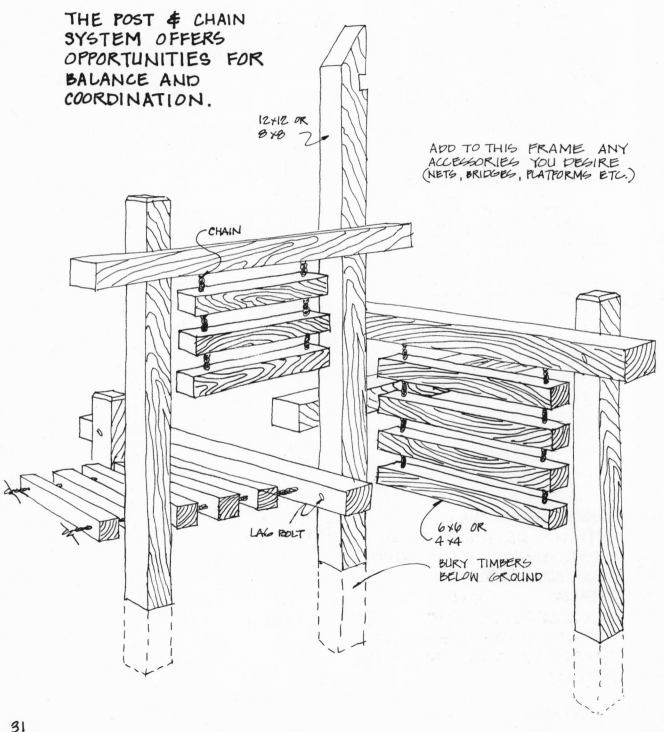

12×12 OR
8×8

ADD TO THIS FRAME ANY
ACCESSORIES YOU DESIRE
(NETS, BRIDGES, PLATFORMS ETC.)

CHAIN

LAG BOLT

6×6 OR
4×4

BURY TIMBERS
BELOW GROUND

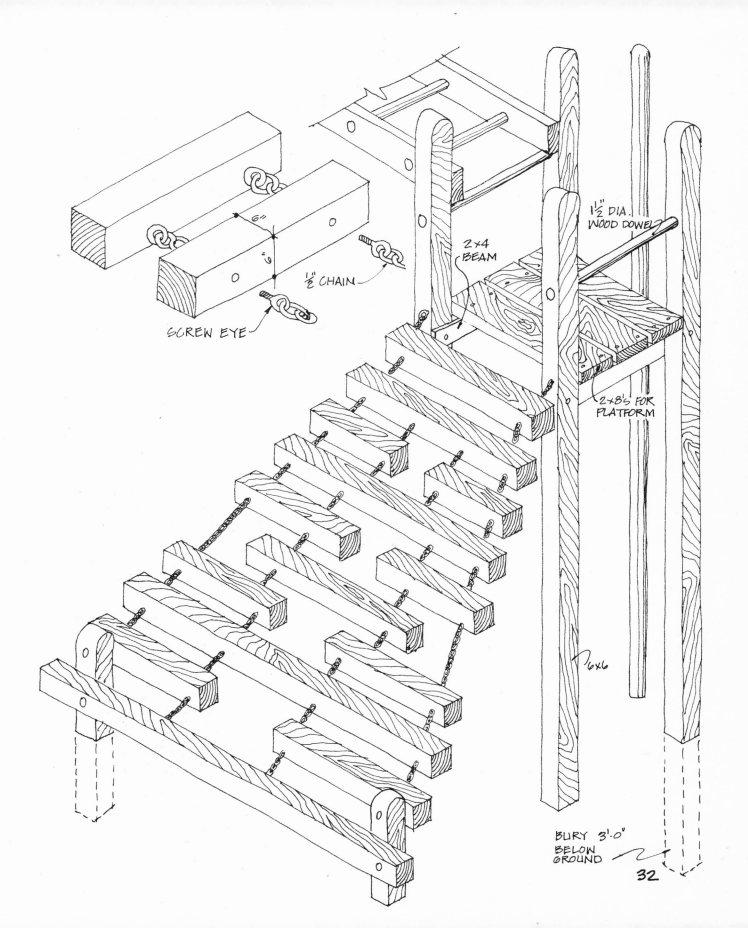

SCREW EYE

6"

6"

1½" CHAIN

2×4 BEAM

1½" DIA. WOOD DOWEL

2×8's FOR PLATFORM

6×6

BURY 3'-0" BELOW GROUND

32

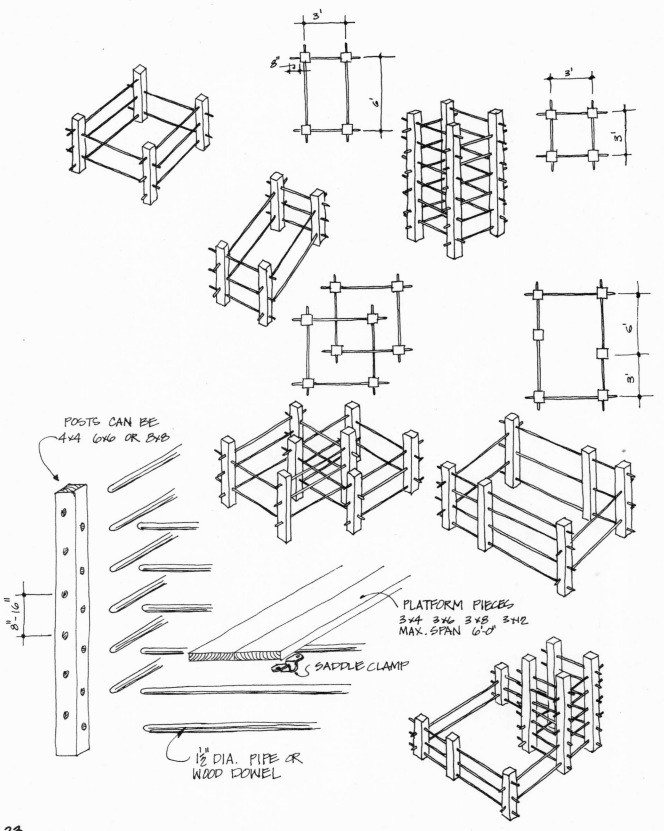

POSTS CAN BE
4x4 6x6 OR 8x8

8"-16"

1½" DIA. PIPE OR
WOOD DOWEL

PLATFORM PIECES
3x4 3x6 3x8 3x12
MAX. SPAN 6'-0"

SADDLE CLAMP

3'

8"

6'

3'

3'

6'

3'

POST AND DOWEL

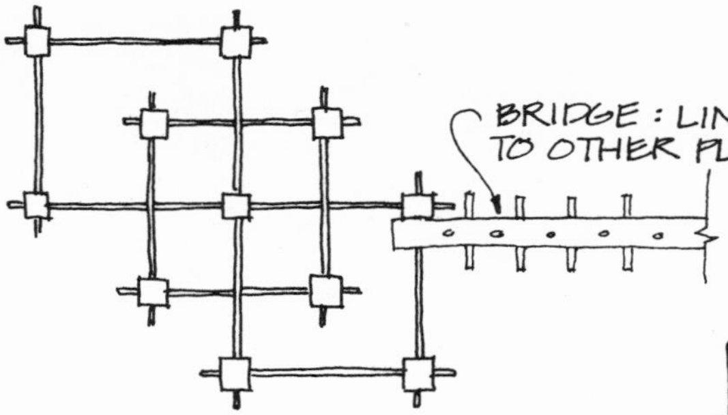

BRIDGE: LINK
TO OTHER PLAY AREAS

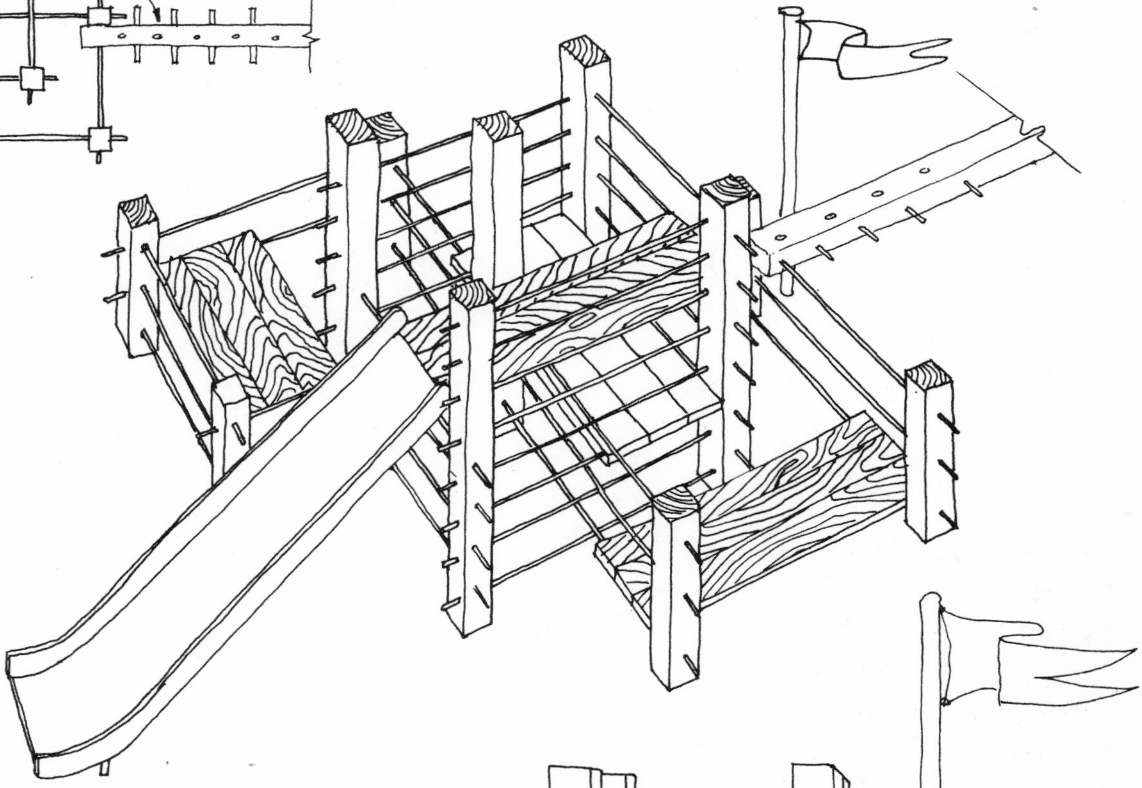

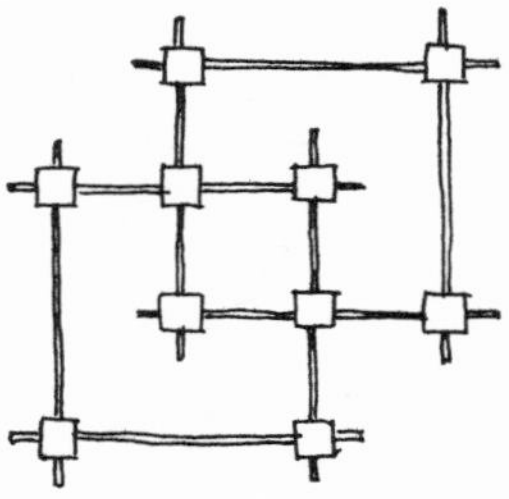

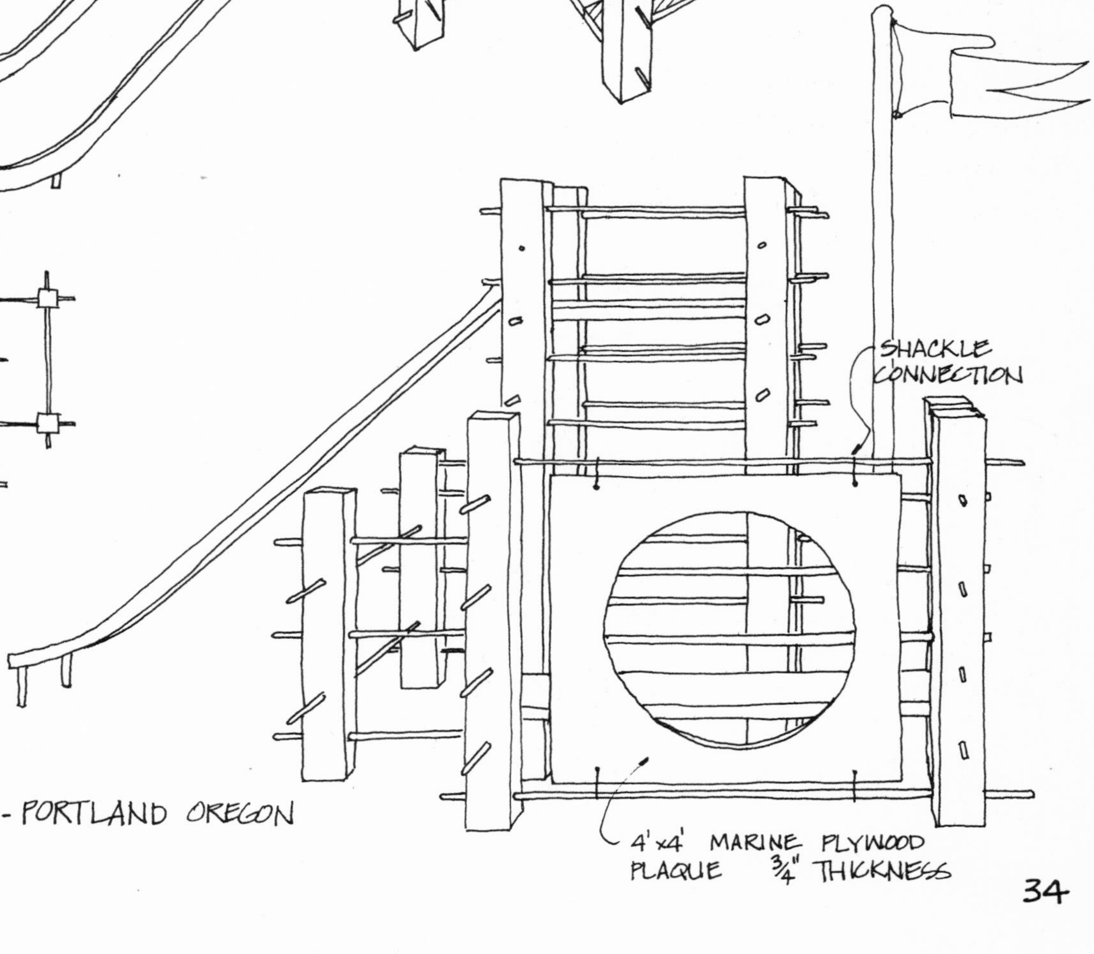

SHACKLE
CONNECTION

*TIMBERFORM - PORTLAND OREGON

4'x4' MARINE PLYWOOD
PLAQUE 3/4" THICKNESS

34

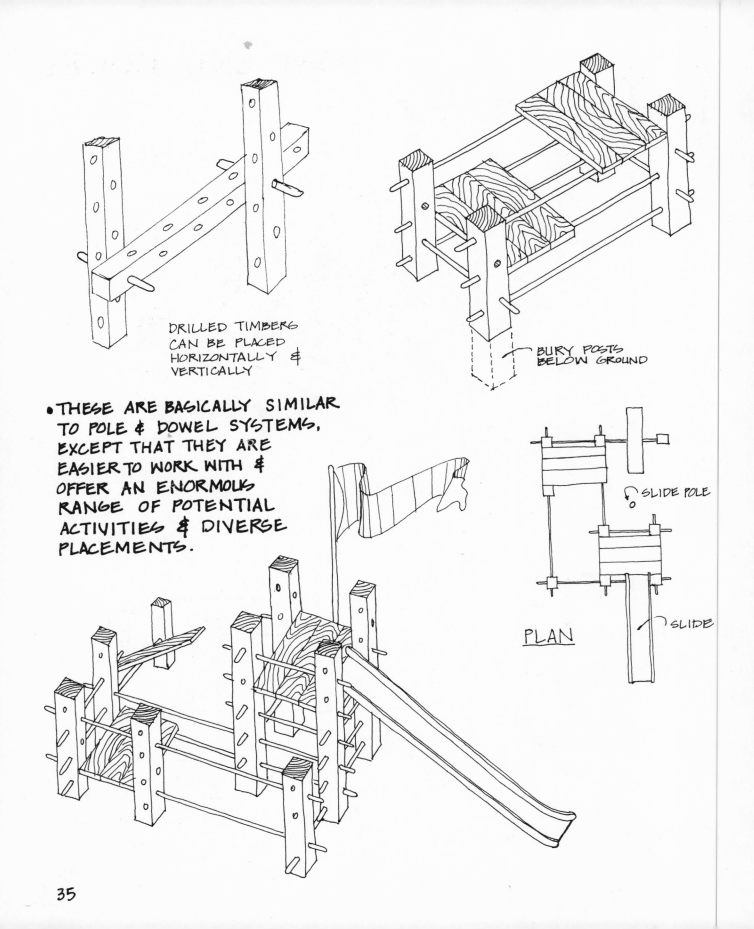

DRILLED TIMBERS
CAN BE PLACED
HORIZONTALLY &
VERTICALLY

BURY POSTS
BELOW GROUND

• THESE ARE BASICALLY SIMILAR
TO POLE & DOWEL SYSTEMS,
EXCEPT THAT THEY ARE
EASIER TO WORK WITH &
OFFER AN ENORMOUS
RANGE OF POTENTIAL
ACTIVITIES & DIVERSE
PLACEMENTS.

SLIDE POLE

PLAN

SLIDE

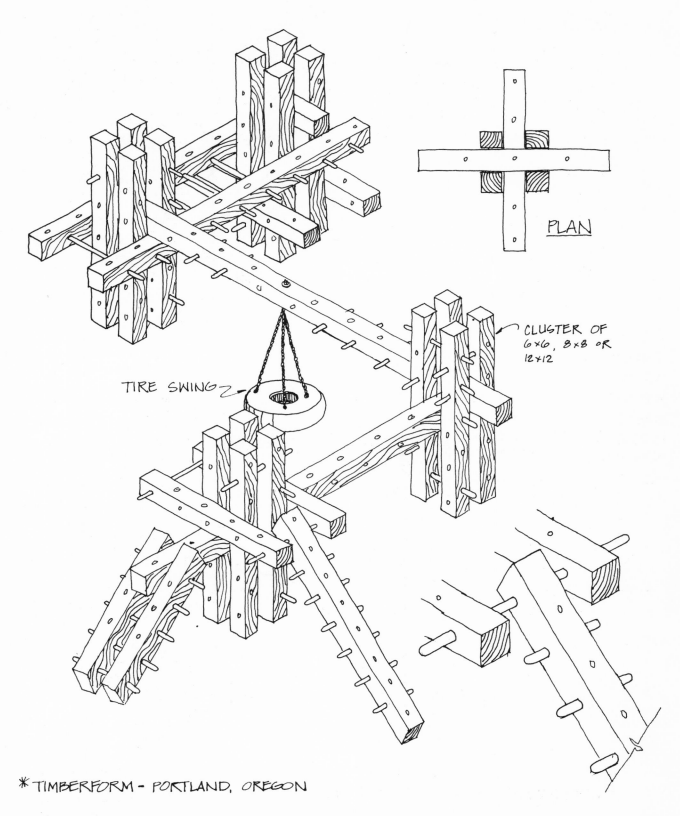

PLAN

CLUSTER OF
6×6, 8×8 OR
12×12

TIRE SWING

*TIMBERFORM - PORTLAND, OREGON

36

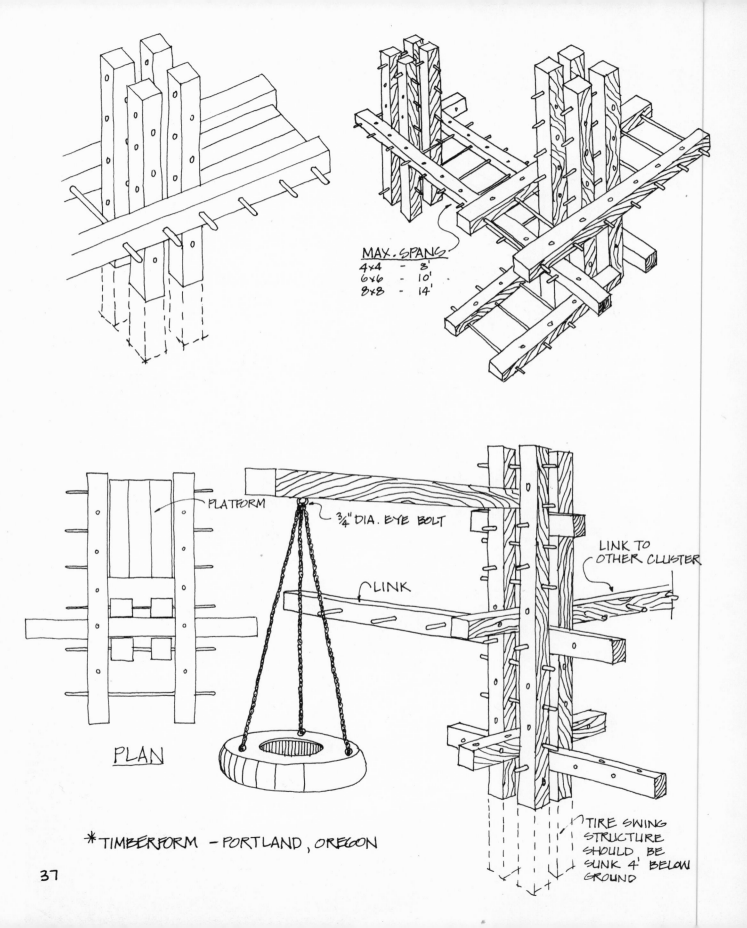

MAX. SPANS
4×4 - 8'
6×6 - 10'
8×8 - 14'

PLATFORM

3/4" DIA. EYE BOLT

LINK

LINK TO
OTHER CLUSTER

PLAN

*TIMBERFORM - PORTLAND, OREGON

TIRE SWING
STRUCTURE
SHOULD BE
SUNK 4' BELOW
GROUND

NOTES

BOTH THE SIDES AND TOPS OF ALL WOOD EDGES SHOULD BE CHAMFERED OR ROUNDED A MIN. OF $\frac{1}{4}$", AND SOMETIMES AS MUCH AS 1". SAND ALL ROUGH SPOTS AND ELIMINATE ALL LARGE SPLINTERED AREAS.

WOOD WILL CONTINUE TO CHECK AND SHRINK, BUT AS LONG AS THERE ARE NO MAJOR SPLINTER AREAS, CHILDREN WILL DEVELOP A SENSE OF DISCRETION AND USE CAUTION.

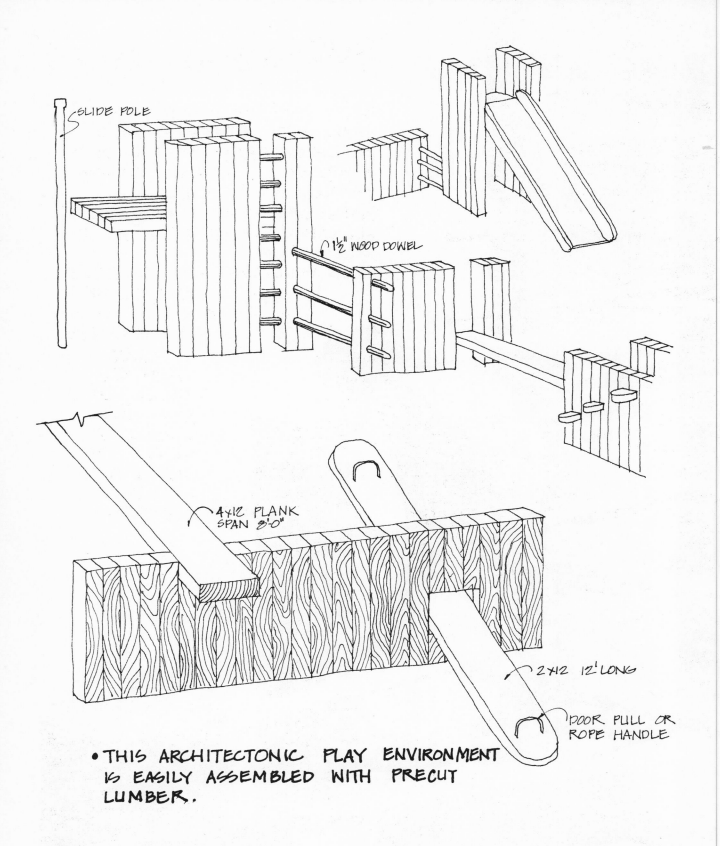

SLIDE POLE

1½" WOOD DOWEL

4×12 PLANK
SPAN 8'0"

2×12 12' LONG

DOOR PULL OR
ROPE HANDLE

• THIS ARCHITECTONIC PLAY ENVIRONMENT
IS EASILY ASSEMBLED WITH PRECUT
LUMBER.

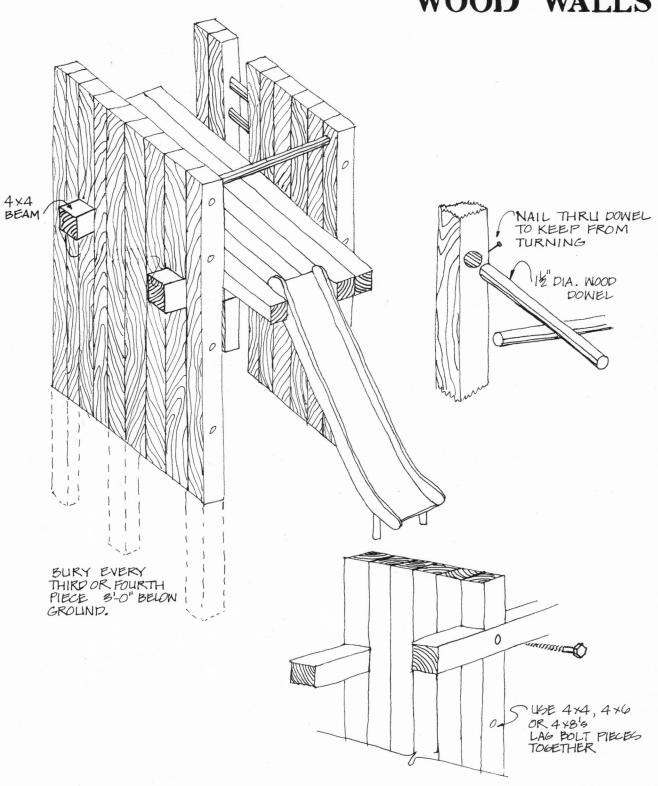

4x4
BEAM

NAIL THRU DOWEL
TO KEEP FROM
TURNING

1½" DIA. WOOD
DOWEL

BURY EVERY
THIRD OR FOURTH
PIECE 3'-0" BELOW
GROUND.

USE 4x4, 4x6
OR 4x8's
LAG BOLT PIECES
TOGETHER

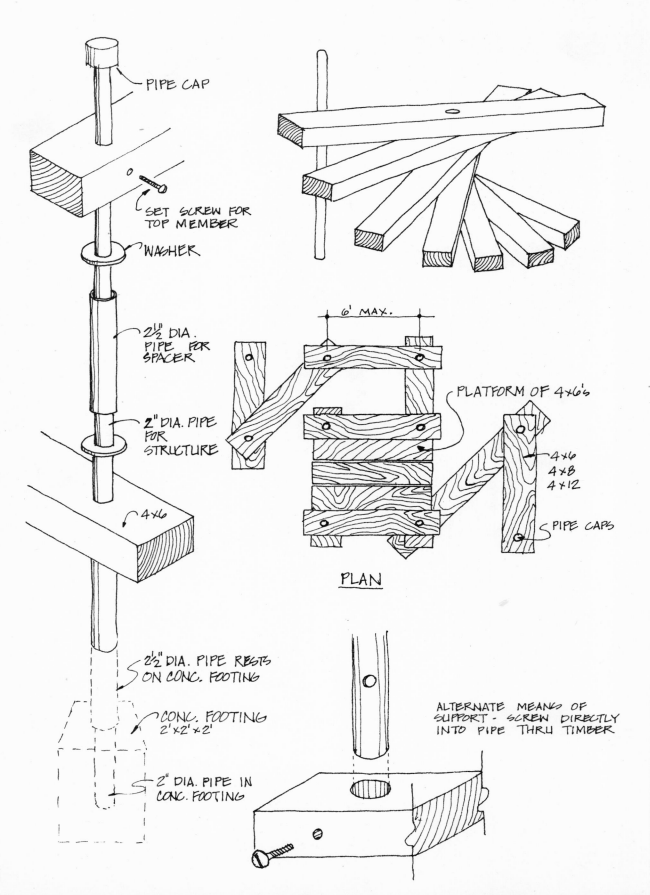

PIPE CAP

SET SCREW FOR TOP MEMBER

WASHER

2½" DIA. PIPE FOR SPACER

2" DIA. PIPE FOR STRUCTURE

4×6

2½" DIA. PIPE RESTS ON CONC. FOOTING

CONC. FOOTING 2'×2'×2'

2" DIA. PIPE IN CONC. FOOTING

6' MAX.

PLATFORM OF 4×6's

4×6
4×8
4×12

PIPE CAPS

PLAN

ALTERNATE MEANS OF SUPPORT - SCREW DIRECTLY INTO PIPE THRU TIMBER

41

POST AND PIPE

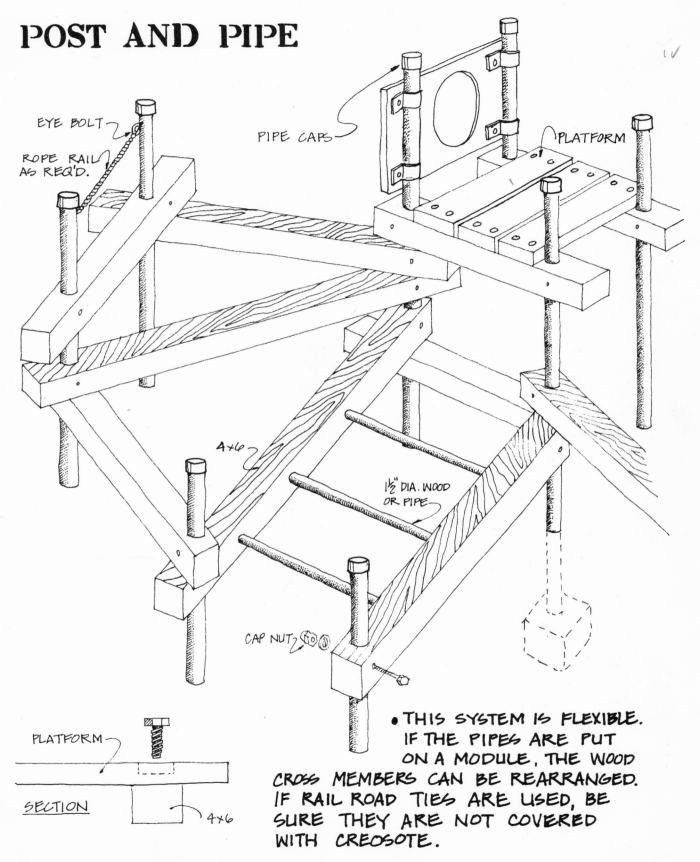

EYE BOLT

ROPE RAIL AS REQ'D.

PIPE CAPS

PLATFORM

4×6

1½" DIA. WOOD OR PIPE

CAP NUT

PLATFORM

SECTION

4×6

• THIS SYSTEM IS FLEXIBLE. IF THE PIPES ARE PUT ON A MODULE, THE WOOD CROSS MEMBERS CAN BE REARRANGED. IF RAIL ROAD TIES ARE USED, BE SURE THEY ARE NOT COVERED WITH CREOSOTE.

42

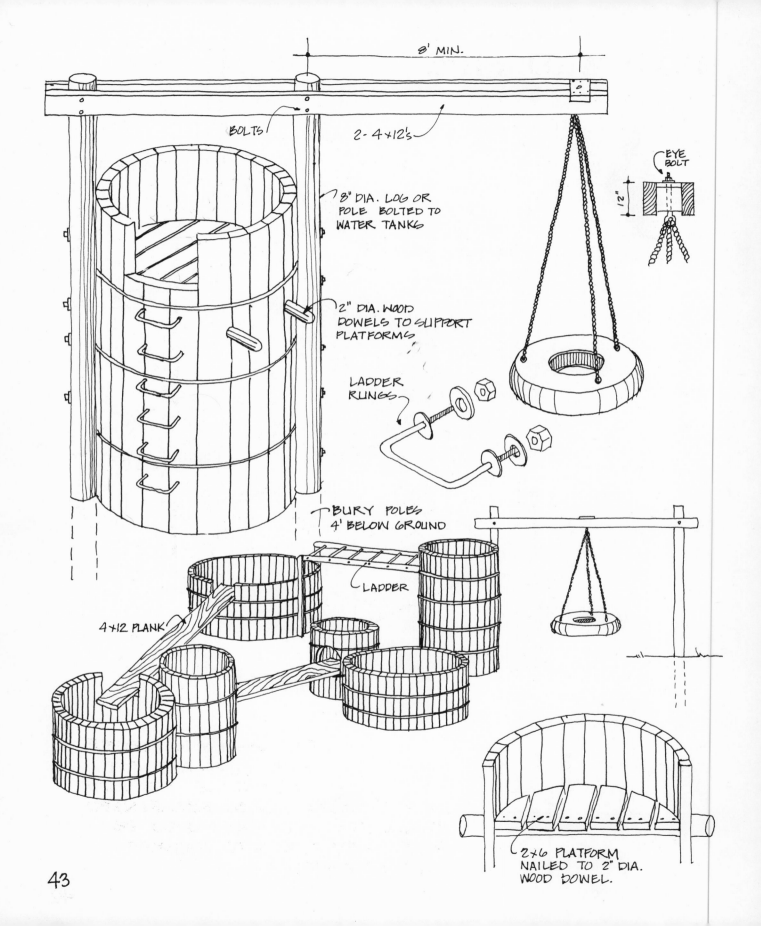

8' MIN.

BOLTS

2- 4×12's

8" DIA. LOG OR
POLE BOLTED TO
WATER TANKS

2" DIA. WOOD
DOWELS TO SUPPORT
PLATFORMS

EYE
BOLT

12"

LADDER
RUNGS

BURY POLES
4' BELOW GROUND

LADDER

4×12 PLANK

2×6 PLATFORM
NAILED TO 2" DIA.
WOOD DOWEL.

43

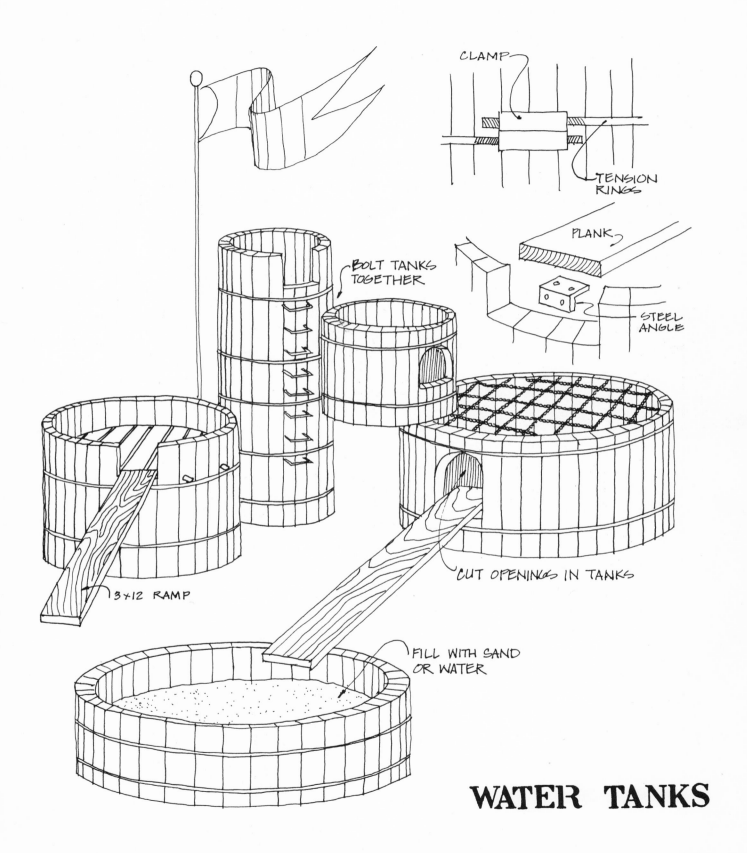

CLAMP

TENSION RINGS

PLANK

STEEL ANGLE

BOLT TANKS TOGETHER

3×12 RAMP

CUT OPENINGS IN TANKS

FILL WITH SAND OR WATER

WATER TANKS

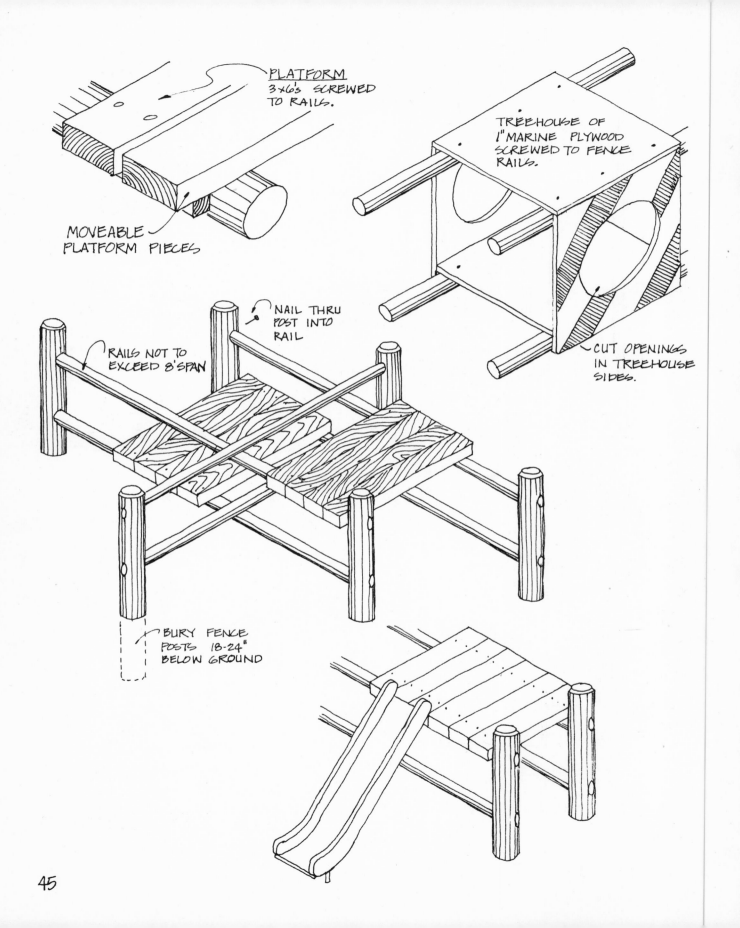

PLATFORM
3x6's SCREWED
TO RAILS.

MOVEABLE
PLATFORM PIECES

TREEHOUSE OF
1" MARINE PLYWOOD
SCREWED TO FENCE
RAILS.

CUT OPENINGS
IN TREEHOUSE
SIDES.

NAIL THRU
POST INTO
RAIL

RAILS NOT TO
EXCEED 8' SPAN

BURY FENCE
POSTS 18-24"
BELOW GROUND

FENCE

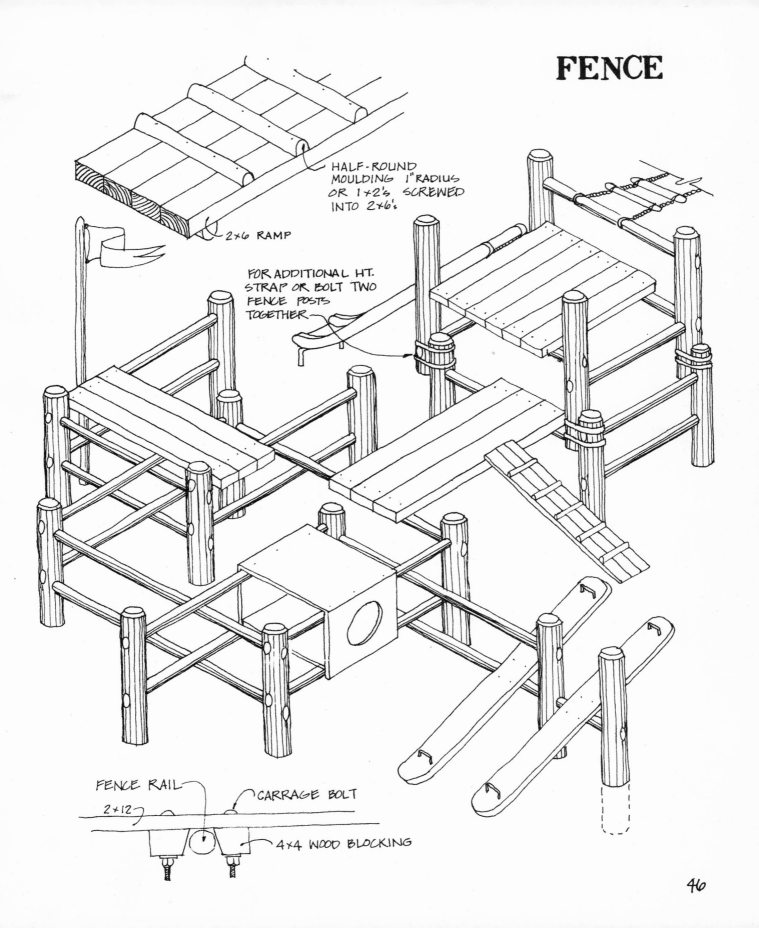

HALF-ROUND MOULDING 1" RADIUS OR 1×2's SCREWED INTO 2×6's

2×6 RAMP

FOR ADDITIONAL HT. STRAP OR BOLT TWO FENCE POSTS TOGETHER

FENCE RAIL

2×12

CARRAGE BOLT

4×4 WOOD BLOCKING

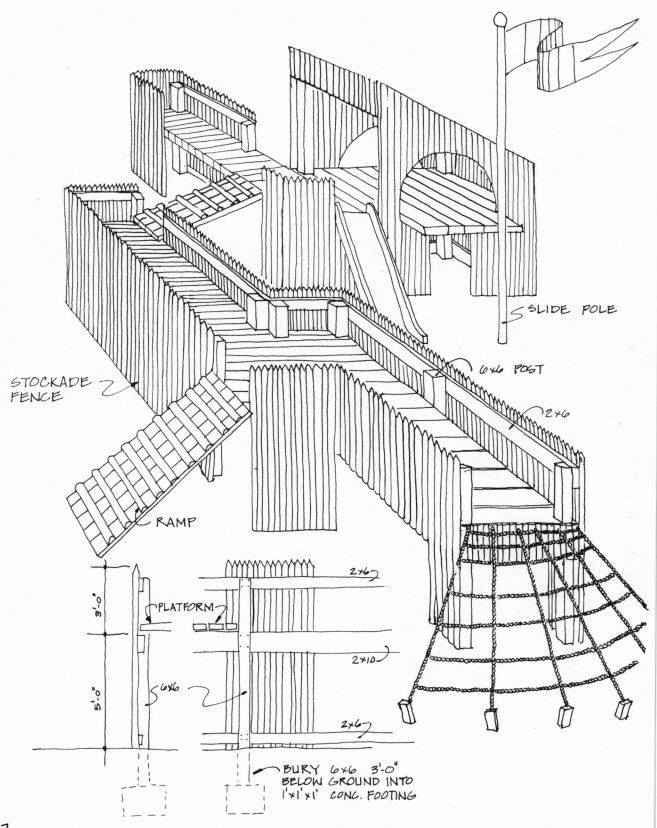

SLIDE POLE

6×6 POST

2×6

STOCKADE
FENCE

RAMP

2×6

3'-0"

PLATFORM

2×10

5'-0"

6×6

2×6

BURY 6×6 3'-0"
BELOW GROUND INTO
1'×1'×1' CONC. FOOTING

47

- FENCING PROVIDES A PLAY AREA AT MINIMAL COST. STOCKADE FENCE SYSTEMS STIMULATE FANTASIES ASSOCIATED WITH OLD FORTS.

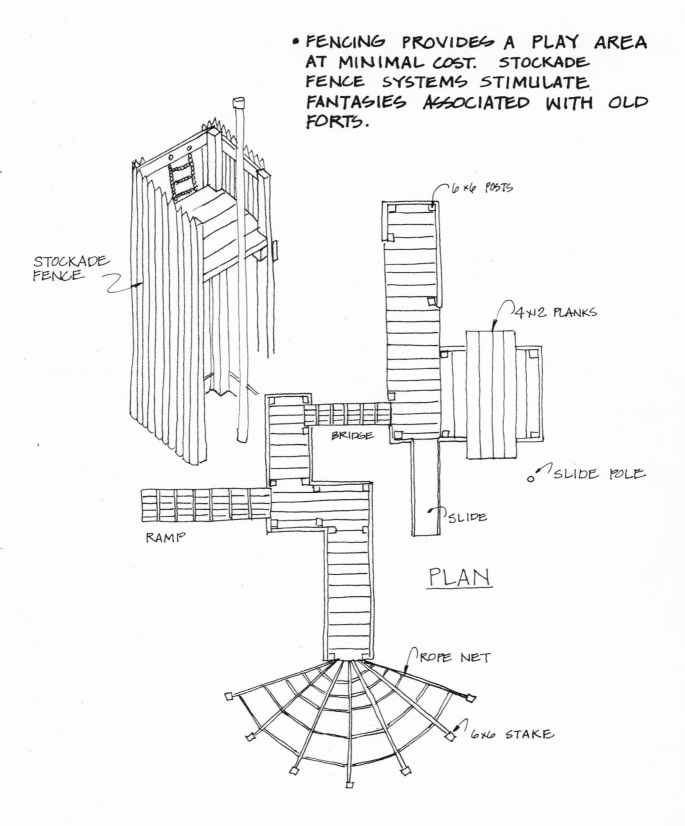

STOCKADE FENCE

6 x 6 POSTS

4 x 12 PLANKS

BRIDGE

SLIDE POLE

SLIDE

RAMP

PLAN

ROPE NET

6 x 6 STAKE

STACKED TIMBERS

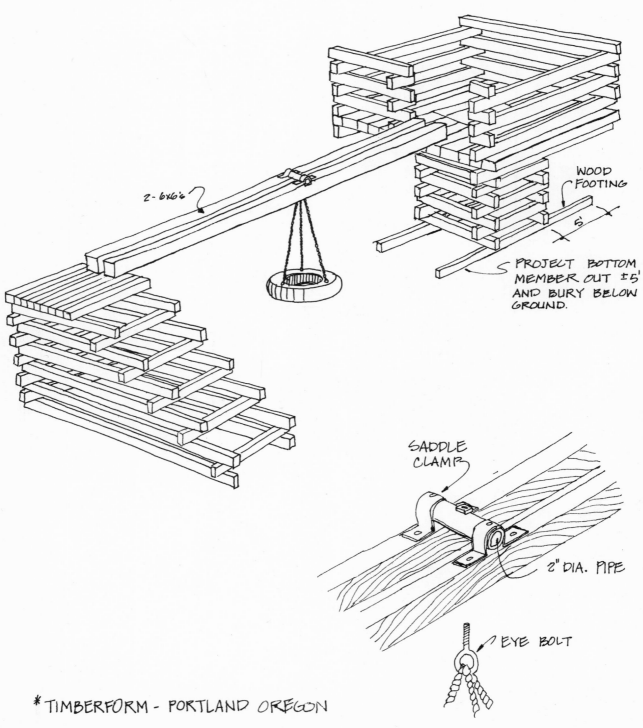

2 - 6x6's

WOOD FOOTING

PROJECT BOTTOM MEMBER OUT ±5' AND BURY BELOW GROUND.

SADDLE CLAMP

2" DIA. PIPE

EYE BOLT

* TIMBERFORM - PORTLAND OREGON

49

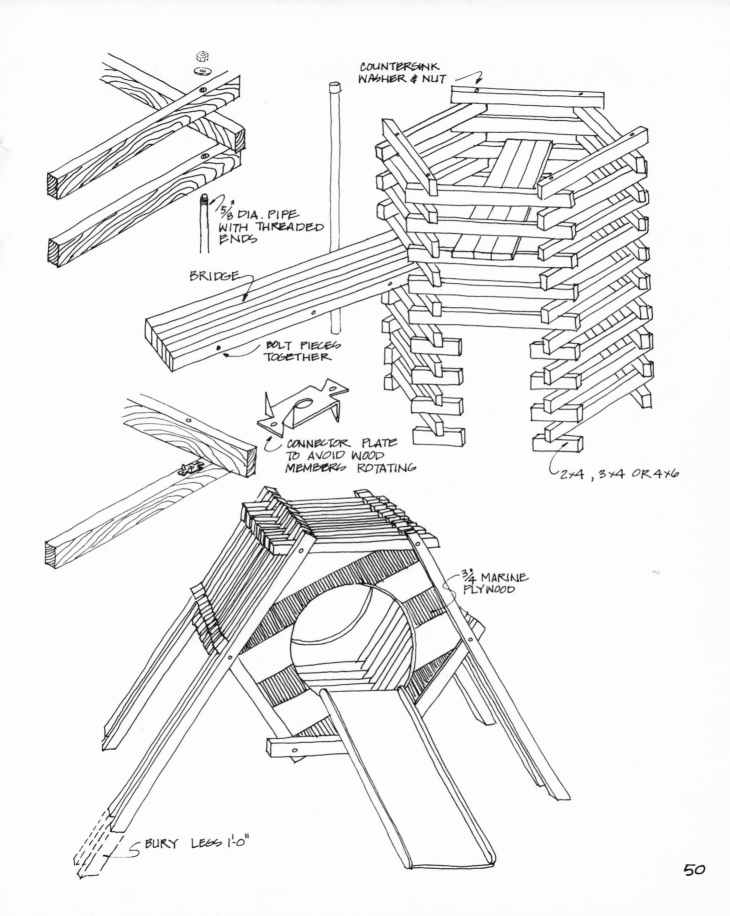

COUNTERSINK WASHER & NUT

5/8" DIA. PIPE WITH THREADED ENDS

BRIDGE

BOLT PIECES TOGETHER

CONNECTOR PLATE TO AVOID WOOD MEMBERS ROTATING

2×4, 3×4 OR 4×6

3/4" MARINE PLYWOOD

BURY LEGS 1'-0"

50

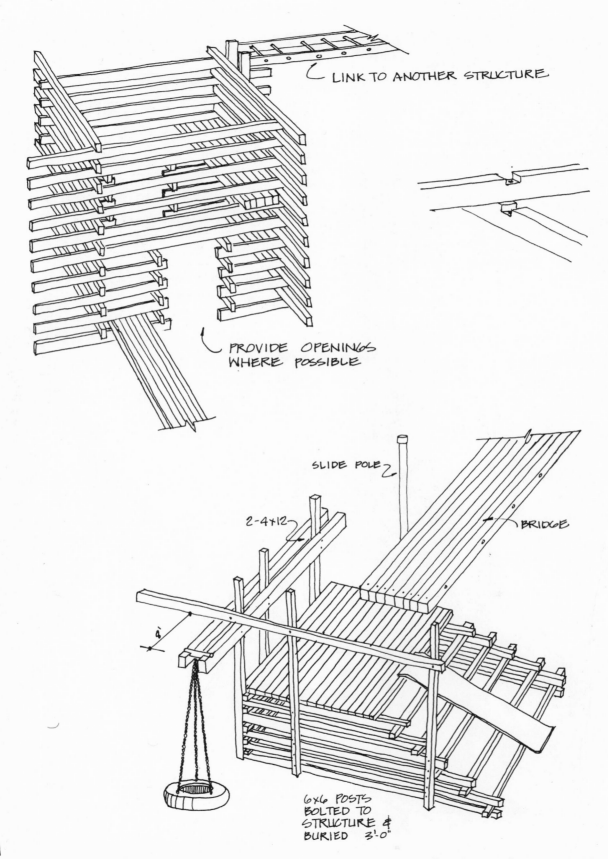

LINK TO ANOTHER STRUCTURE

PROVIDE OPENINGS
WHERE POSSIBLE

SLIDE POLE

BRIDGE

2-4×12

4"

6×6 POSTS
BOLTED TO
STRUCTURE &
BURIED 3'-0"

51

STACKED TIMBERS ARE MADE FROM 2×4's , 3×4's , 4×6's -
THE SIZE DEPENDS UPON THE DESIRED SCALE. THE
LARGER MEMBERS ARE RECOMMENDED FOR INSTITUTIONAL
USE.

THIS IS ESSENTIALLY A VERY SIMPLE SYSTEM IN WHICH
EACH ELEMENT CAN BE HELD TOGETHER BY A CONTINUOUS
PIPE, OR ONE CROSSMEMBER CAN BE LAG BOLTED INTO
THE OTHERS. RACKING CAN BE A PROBLEM AND PREVENT-
ATIVE MEASURES SHOULD BE TAKEN. USING METAL
BRACES, NOTCHING EACH PIECE INTO THE OTHERS, OR
DOUBLE BOLTING ARE ALL SOLUTIONS.

THESE STRUCTURES ARE STURDY AND REQUIRE NO
FOOTINGS EXCEPT IN CASES WHERE THE TOP
IS GREATER THAN THE BOTTOM. IN THESE
SITUATIONS THE BOTTOM RAIL SHOULD BE
MADE THE SAME LENGTH AS THE TOP AND
PLACED BELOW GRADE.

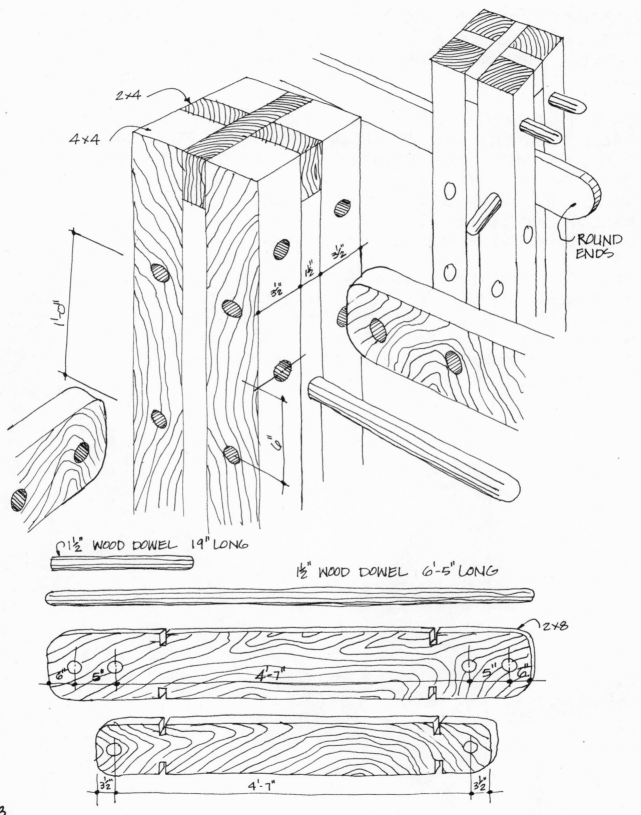

2×4

4×4

1'-0"

$3\frac{1}{2}$"

$1\frac{1}{2}$"

$3\frac{1}{2}$"

6"

ROUND
ENDS

$1\frac{1}{2}$" WOOD DOWEL 19" LONG

$1\frac{1}{2}$" WOOD DOWEL 6'-5" LONG

2×8

6" 5"

5" 6"

4'-7"

$3\frac{1}{2}$"

4'-7"

$3\frac{1}{2}$"

53

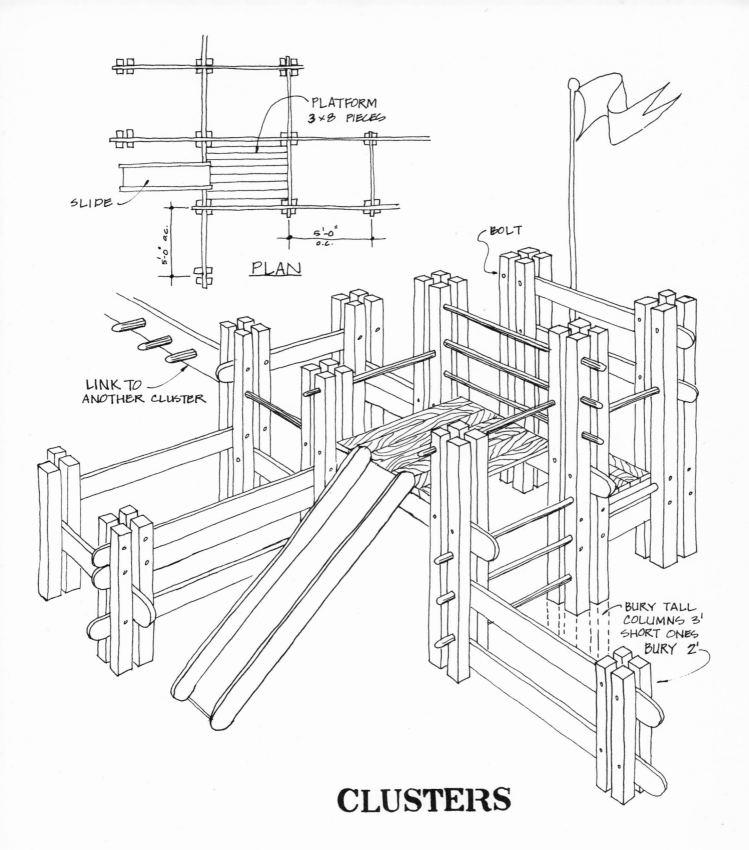

PLATFORM
3 × 8 PIECES

SLIDE

5'-0" o.c.

5'-0" o.c.

PLAN

BOLT

LINK TO
ANOTHER CLUSTER

BURY TALL
COLUMNS 3'
SHORT ONES
BURY 2'

CLUSTERS

EARTH WORK

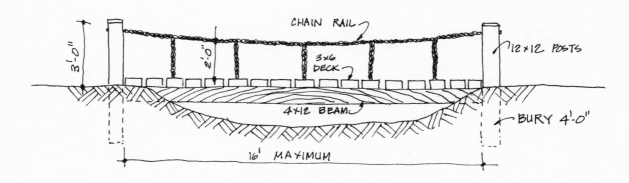

CHAIN RAIL

3'-0"

2'-0"

3×6
DECK

12×12 POSTS

4×12 BEAM

BURY 4'-0"

16' MAXIMUM

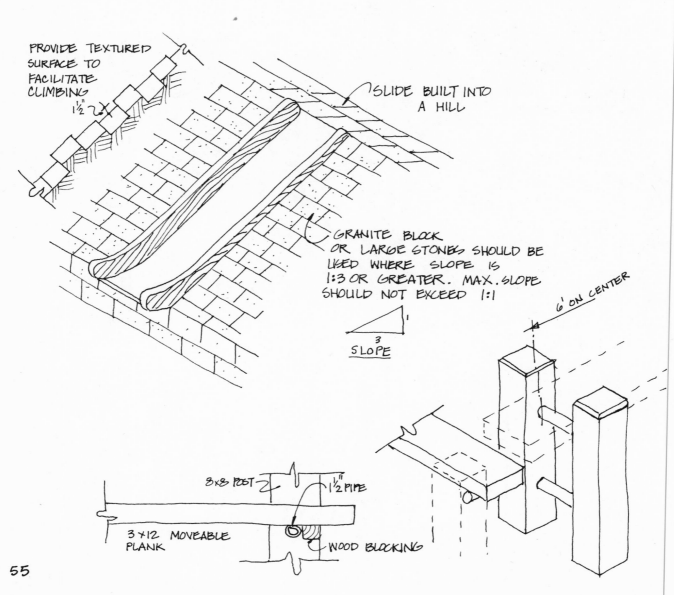

PROVIDE TEXTURED
SURFACE TO
FACILITATE
CLIMBING

1½"

SLIDE BUILT INTO
A HILL

GRANITE BLOCK
OR LARGE STONES SHOULD BE
USED WHERE SLOPE IS
1:3 OR GREATER. MAX. SLOPE
SHOULD NOT EXCEED 1:1

3
1
SLOPE

6' ON CENTER

8×8 POST

1½" PIPE

3×12 MOVEABLE
PLANK

WOOD BLOCKING

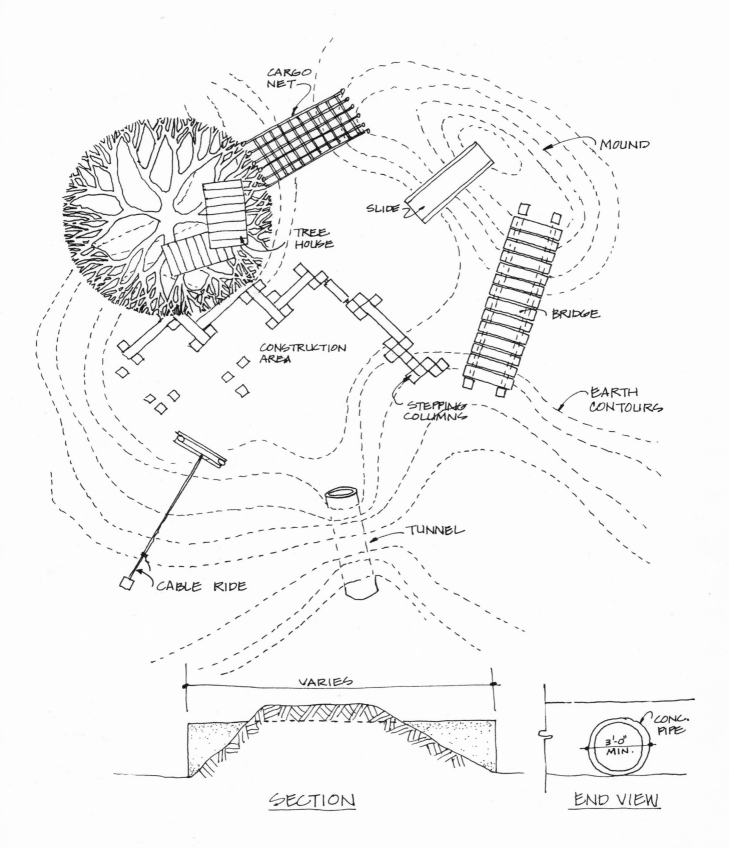

CARGO NET

MOUND

SLIDE

TREE HOUSE

BRIDGE

CONSTRUCTION AREA

STEPPING COLUMNS

EARTH CONTOURS

TUNNEL

CABLE RIDE

VARIES

SECTION

CONC. PIPE

3'-0" MIN.

END VIEW

56

NETS

ROPE

SNAP HOOK

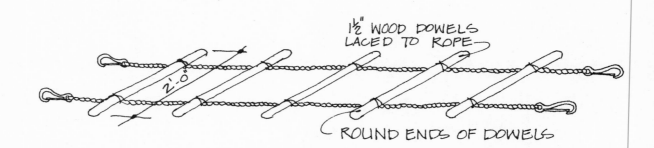

1½" WOOD DOWELS
LACED TO ROPE

2'0"

ROUND ENDS OF DOWELS

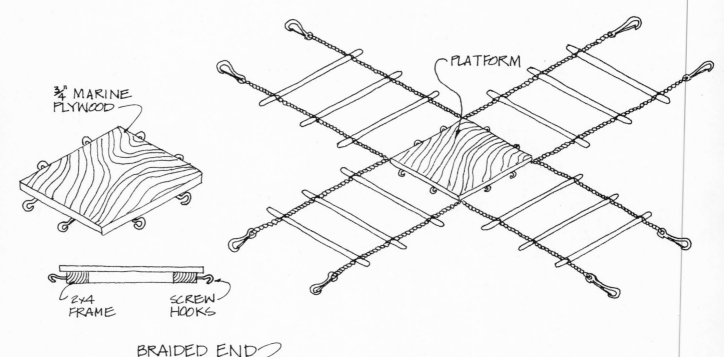

PLATFORM

¾" MARINE
PLYWOOD

2×4
FRAME

SCREW
HOOKS

BRAIDED END

LASHED
END

SNAP HOOK

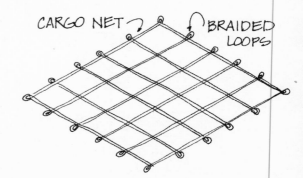

CARGO NET

BRAIDED
LOOPS

57

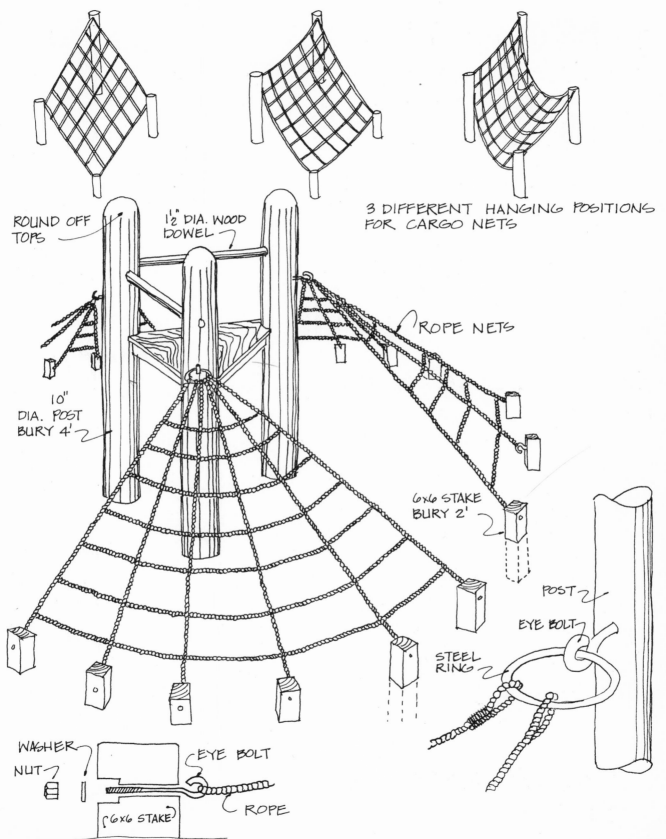

ROUND OFF TOPS

1½" DIA. WOOD DOWEL

3 DIFFERENT HANGING POSITIONS FOR CARGO NETS

ROPE NETS

10" DIA. POST BURY 4'

6x6 STAKE BURY 2'

POST

EYE BOLT

STEEL RING

WASHER

NUT

EYE BOLT

6x6 STAKE

ROPE

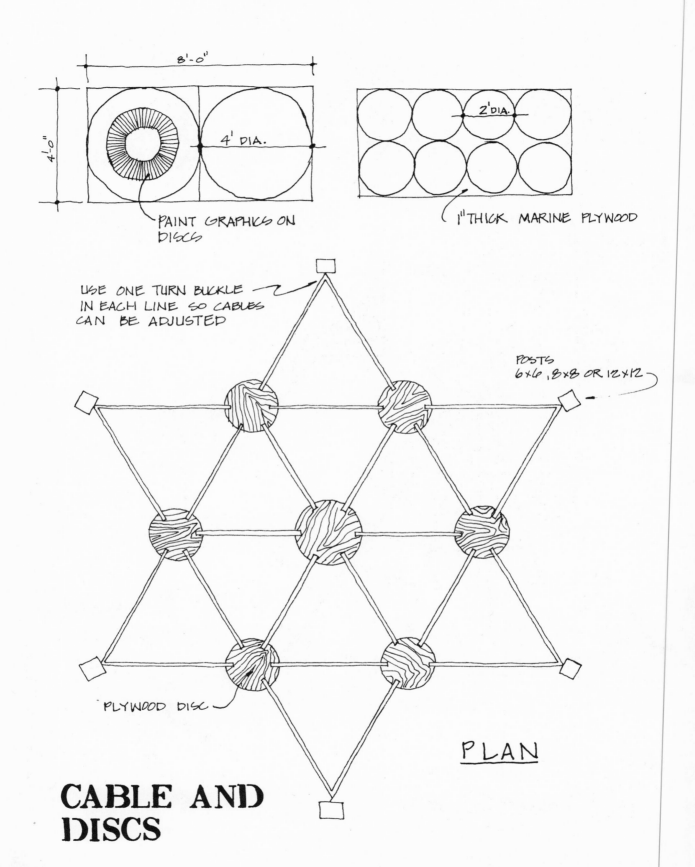

8'-0"

4'-0"

4' DIA.

PAINT GRAPHICS ON
DISCS

2' DIA.

1" THICK MARINE PLYWOOD

USE ONE TURN BUCKLE
IN EACH LINE SO CABLES
CAN BE ADJUSTED

POSTS
6×6, 8×8 OR 12×12

PLYWOOD DISC

PLAN

CABLE AND
DISCS

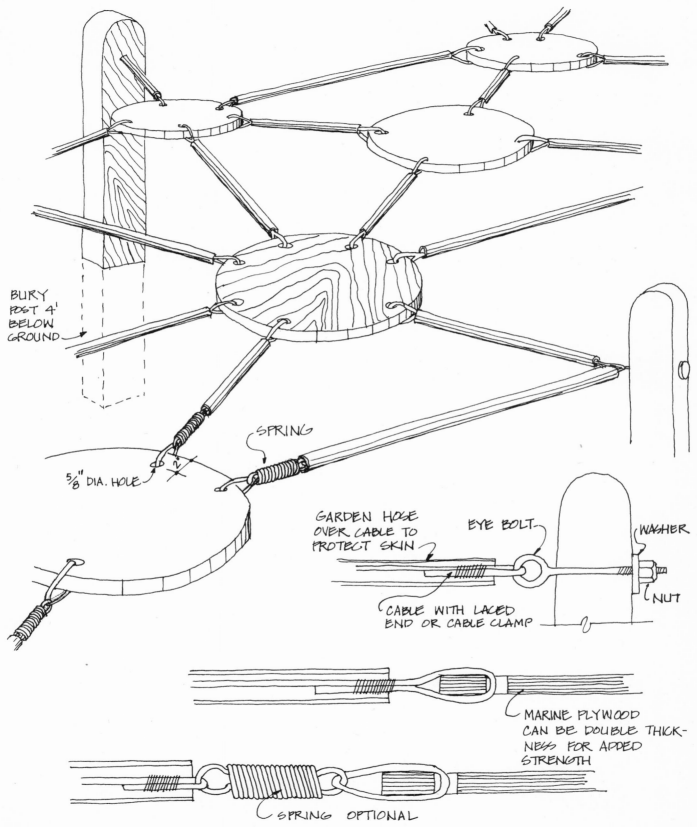

BURY
POST 4'
BELOW
GROUND

SPRING

5/8" DIA. HOLE

2"

GARDEN HOSE
OVER CABLE TO
PROTECT SKIN

EYE BOLT

WASHER

NUT

CABLE WITH LACED
END OR CABLE CLAMP

MARINE PLYWOOD
CAN BE DOUBLE THICK-
NESS FOR ADDED
STRENGTH

SPRING OPTIONAL

60

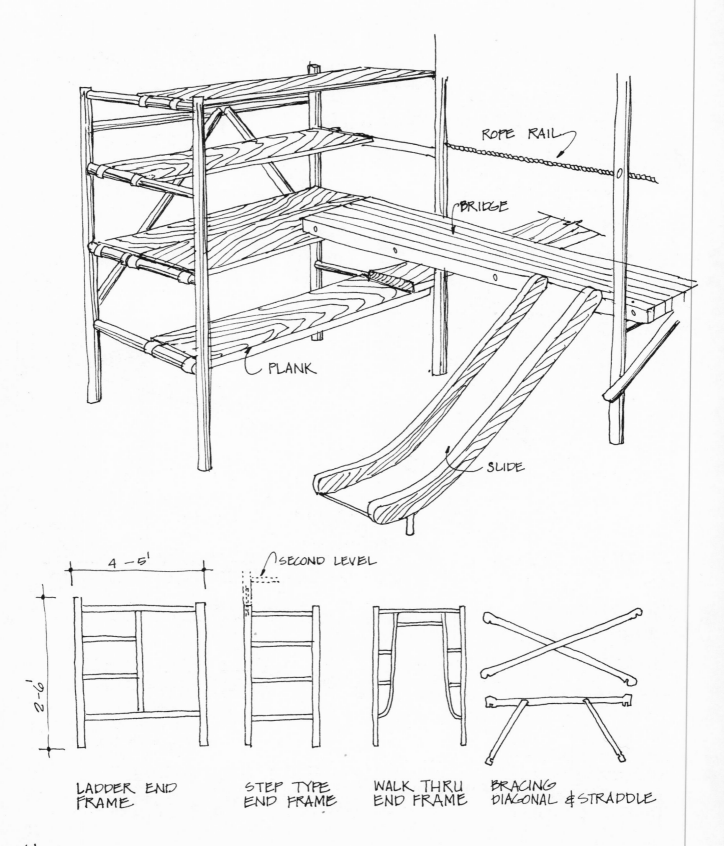

ROPE RAIL

BRIDGE

PLANK

SLIDE

4 — 5'

2'-6"

SECOND LEVEL

LADDER END
FRAME

STEP TYPE
END FRAME

WALK THRU
END FRAME

BRACING
DIAGONAL & STRADDLE

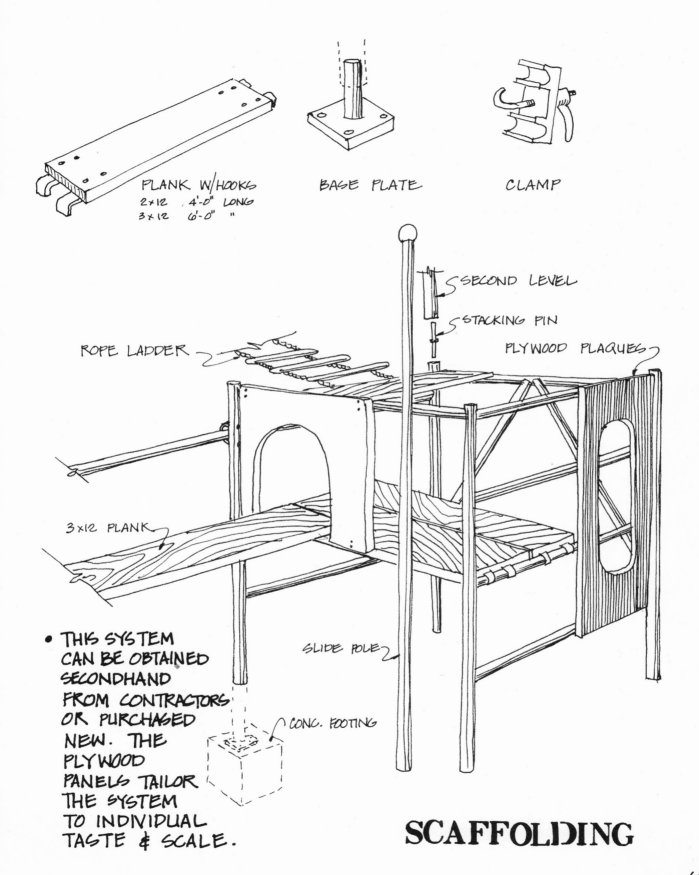

PLANK W/HOOKS
2×12 , 4'-0" LONG
3×12 6'-0" "

BASE PLATE

CLAMP

SECOND LEVEL

STACKING PIN

PLYWOOD PLAQUES

ROPE LADDER

3×12 PLANK

SLIDE POLE

CONC. FOOTING

• THIS SYSTEM
CAN BE OBTAINED
SECONDHAND
FROM CONTRACTORS
OR PURCHASED
NEW. THE
PLYWOOD
PANELS TAILOR
THE SYSTEM
TO INDIVIDUAL
TASTE & SCALE.

SCAFFOLDING

TREE HOUSE

• ONE OF THE MOST MEANINGFUL PLAY FORMS, A TREE HOUSE
PROVIDES CHILDREN WITH A SENSE OF OWNERSHIP AND
STIMULATES IMAGINATION AND FANTASY. DO NOT
BE AFRAID TO BOLT THROUGH A TREE.
PROPER DRILLING AND WOUND
TREATMENTS ELIMINATE THE
POSSIBILITY OF THE TREE DYING.
I DO RECOMMEND, FOR SAFETY,
THAT ROPE RAILINGS BE
USED.

EYE BOLT

LAG BOLT

ROPE RAIL

2×6 DECK
SPAN 4'-0"

2-2×4's
SPAN 6'-0"

NOTES

IF COLOR IS DESIRED, INSTEAD OF
PAINT USE A WOOD STAIN; IT
REQUIRES LESS MAINTENANCE
AND WEATHERS BETTER.

DRUMS

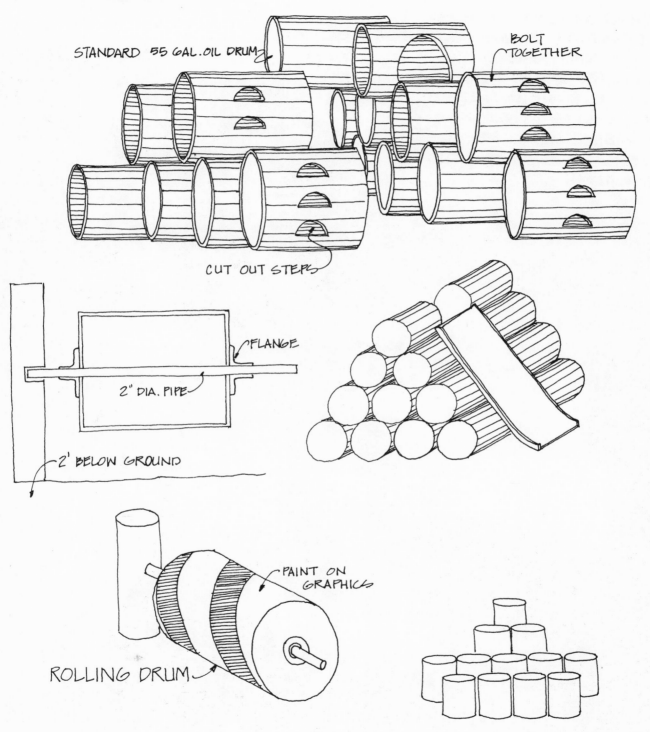

STANDARD 55 GAL. OIL DRUM

BOLT TOGETHER

CUT OUT STEPS

FLANGE

2" DIA. PIPE

2' BELOW GROUND

PAINT ON GRAPHICS

ROLLING DRUM

65

• WHEN AVAILABLE, THESE
VERSATILE DRUMS CAN BE
USED FOR ENCLOSURES,
TUNNELS AND PLATFORMS.
THE FOLLOWING PAGES
ILLUSTRATE DESIGNS
COMBINING DRUMS WITH
OTHER ELEMENTS AND
SYSTEMS.

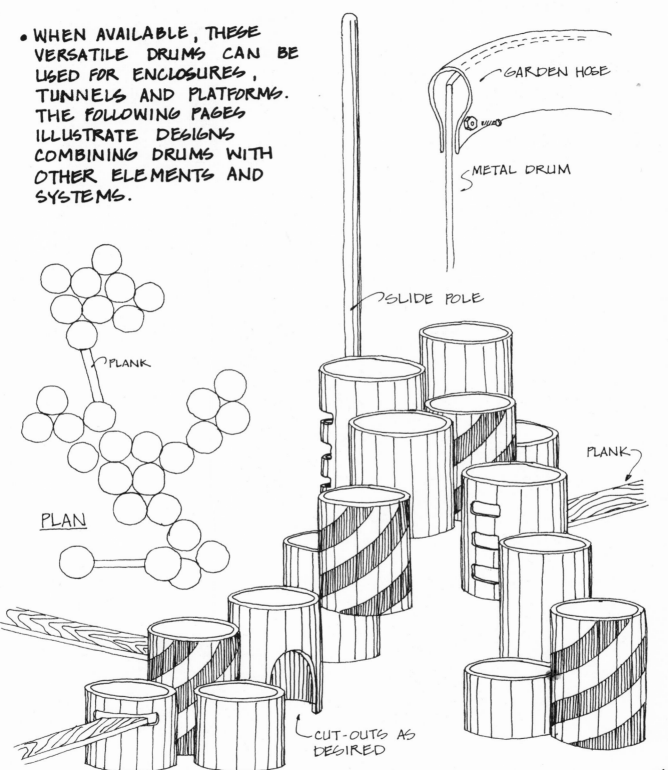

GARDEN HOSE

METAL DRUM

SLIDE POLE

PLANK

PLAN

PLANK

CUT-OUTS AS
DESIRED

60

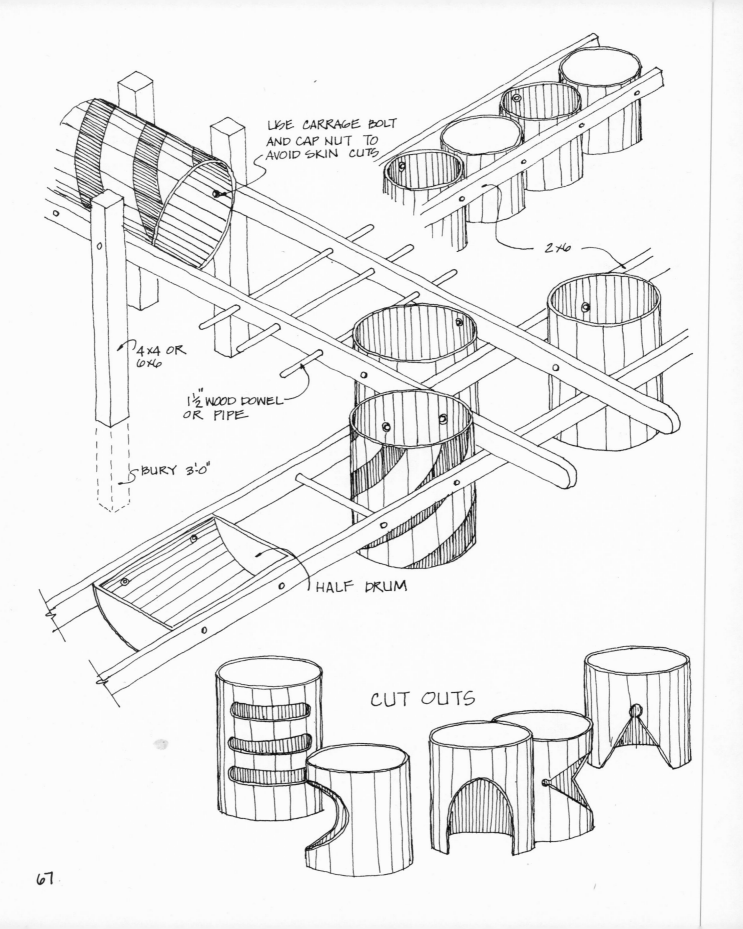

USE CARRAGE BOLT AND CAP NUT TO AVOID SKIN CUTS

2×6

4×4 OR 6×6

BURY 3'-0"

1½" WOOD DOWEL OR PIPE

HALF DRUM

CUT OUTS

67.

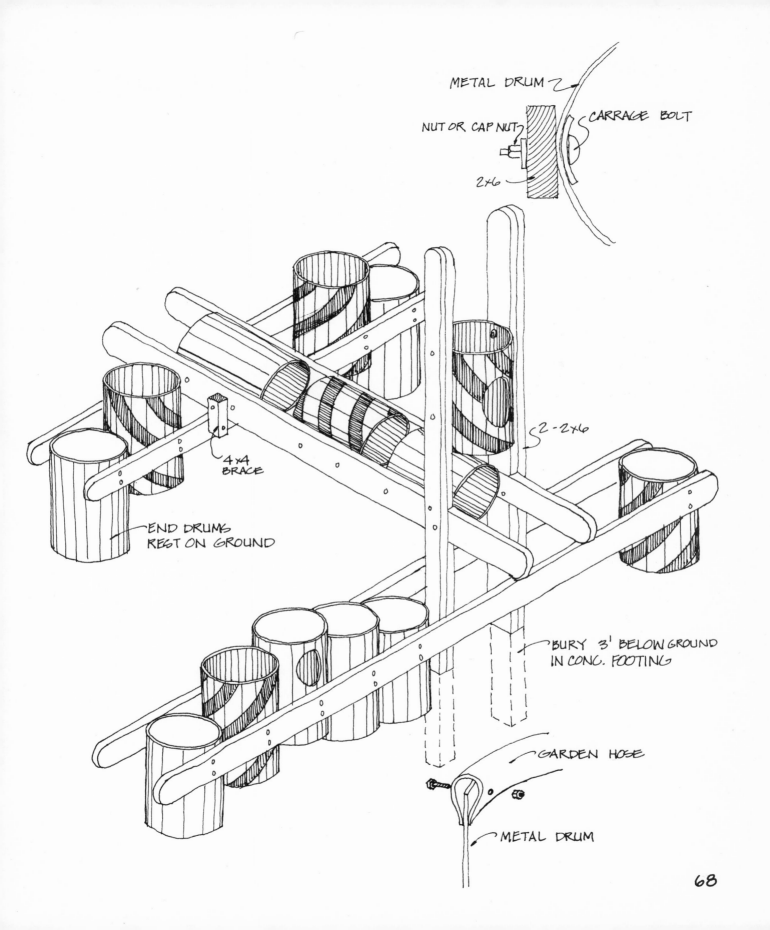

METAL DRUM

CARRIAGE BOLT

NUT OR CAP NUT

2×6

2—2×6

4×4 BRACE

END DRUMS REST ON GROUND

BURY 3' BELOW GROUND IN CONC. FOOTING

GARDEN HOSE

METAL DRUM

68

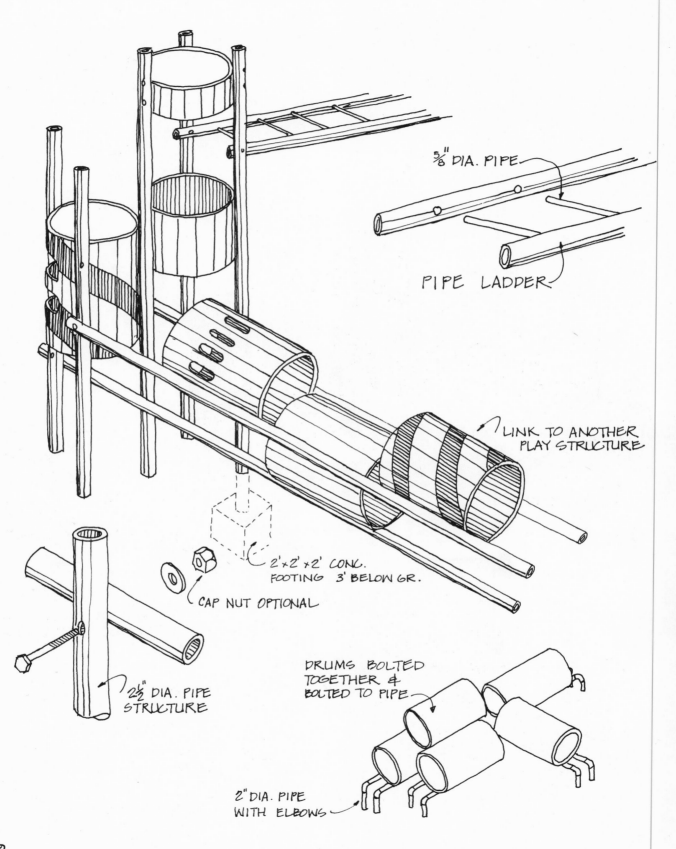

$\frac{5}{8}''$ DIA. PIPE.

PIPE LADDER

LINK TO ANOTHER PLAY STRUCTURE

2'×2'×2' CONC. FOOTING 3' BELOW GR.

CAP NUT OPTIONAL

$2\frac{1}{2}''$ DIA. PIPE STRUCTURE

DRUMS BOLTED TOGETHER & BOLTED TO PIPE

2" DIA. PIPE WITH ELBOWS

69

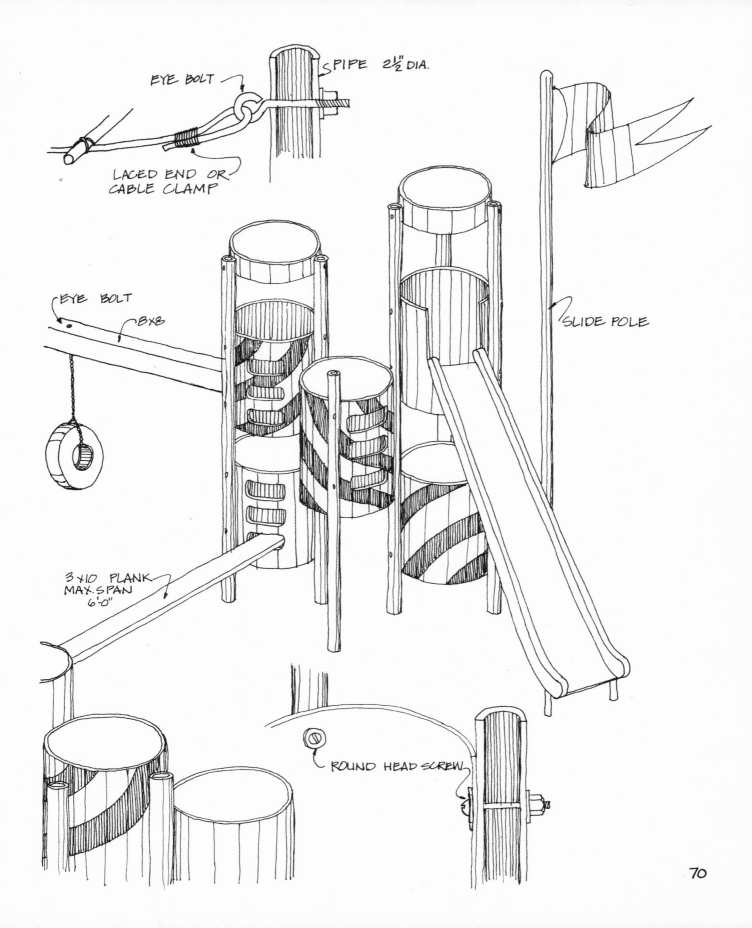

EYE BOLT

SPIPE 2½" DIA.

LACED END OR
CABLE CLAMP

EYE BOLT

8×8

SLIDE POLE

3×10 PLANK
MAX. SPAN
6'-0"

ROUND HEAD SCREW

70

TUBES

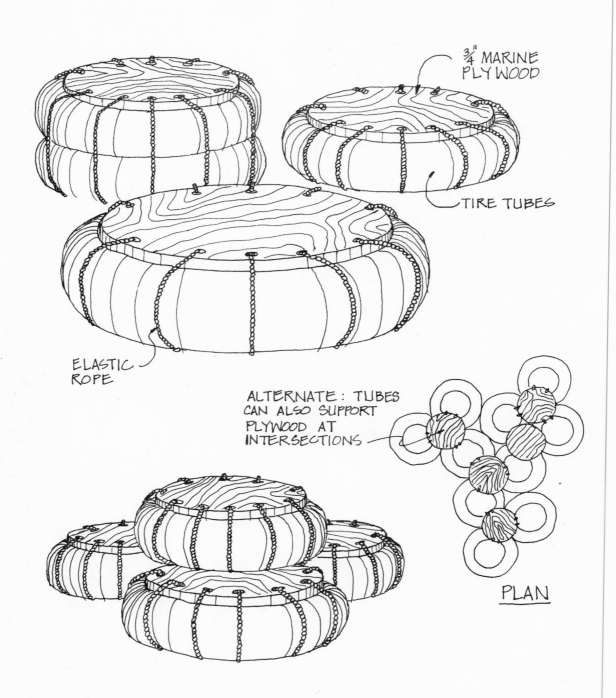

¾" MARINE PLYWOOD

TIRE TUBES

ELASTIC ROPE

ALTERNATE: TUBES CAN ALSO SUPPORT PLYWOOD AT INTERSECTIONS

PLAN

71

NOTES

WHEN USING METAL, REMOVE
RUST FROM ALL SURFACES
AND PAINT WITH AN OUT-
DOOR RUST-RESISTANT
PAINT. USE GALVANIZED
METAL WHEREVER
POSSIBLE, BOTH ON
THE PLAY STRUCTURES
AND WHEN USING
FASTENINGS
AND HARDWARE.

TIRES

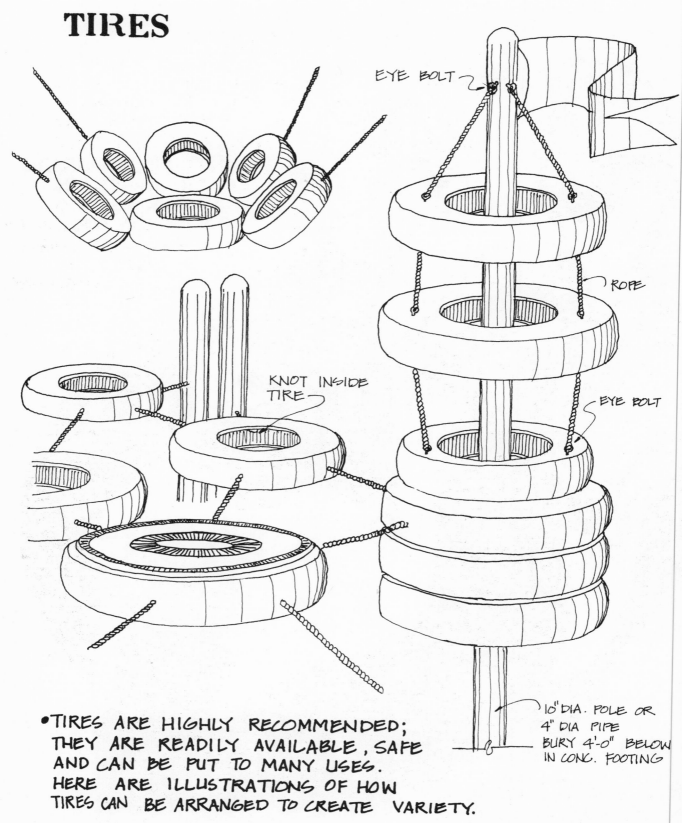

EYE BOLT

ROPE

EYE BOLT

KNOT INSIDE TIRE

10" DIA. POLE OR 4" DIA PIPE BURY 4'-0" BELOW IN CONC. FOOTING

• TIRES ARE HIGHLY RECOMMENDED; THEY ARE READILY AVAILABLE, SAFE AND CAN BE PUT TO MANY USES. HERE ARE ILLUSTRATIONS OF HOW TIRES CAN BE ARRANGED TO CREATE VARIETY.

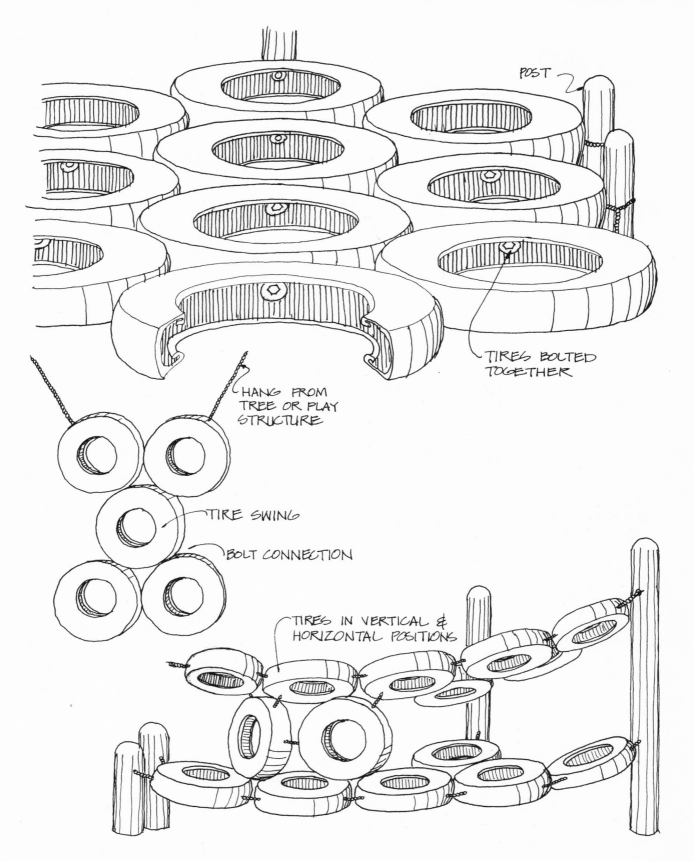

POST

TIRES BOLTED TOGETHER

HANG FROM TREE OR PLAY STRUCTURE

TIRE SWING

BOLT CONNECTION

TIRES IN VERTICAL & HORIZONTAL POSITIONS

74

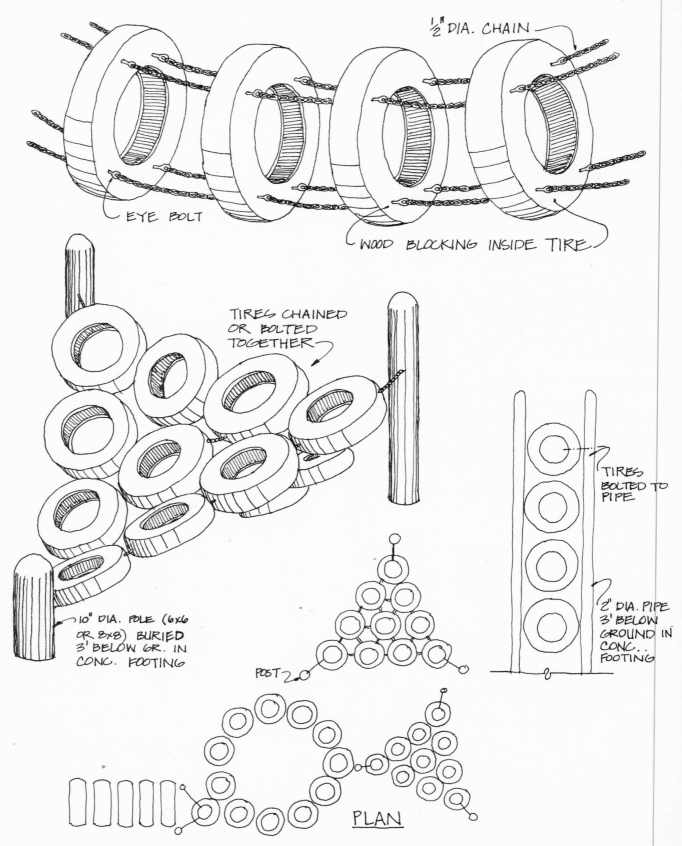

½" DIA. CHAIN

EYE BOLT

WOOD BLOCKING INSIDE TIRE

TIRES CHAINED OR BOLTED TOGETHER

TIRES BOLTED TO PIPE

10" DIA. POLE (6x6 OR 8x8) BURIED 3' BELOW GR. IN CONC. FOOTING

2" DIA. PIPE 3' BELOW GROUND IN CONC. FOOTING

POST

PLAN

75

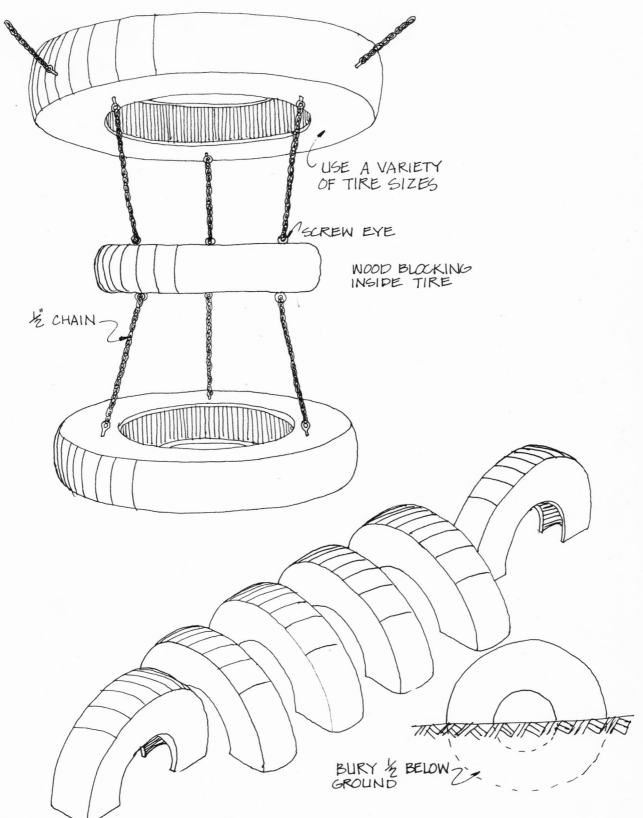

USE A VARIETY
OF TIRE SIZES

SCREW EYE

WOOD BLOCKING
INSIDE TIRE

$\frac{1}{2}$" CHAIN

BURY $\frac{1}{2}$ BELOW
GROUND

76

SPOOLS

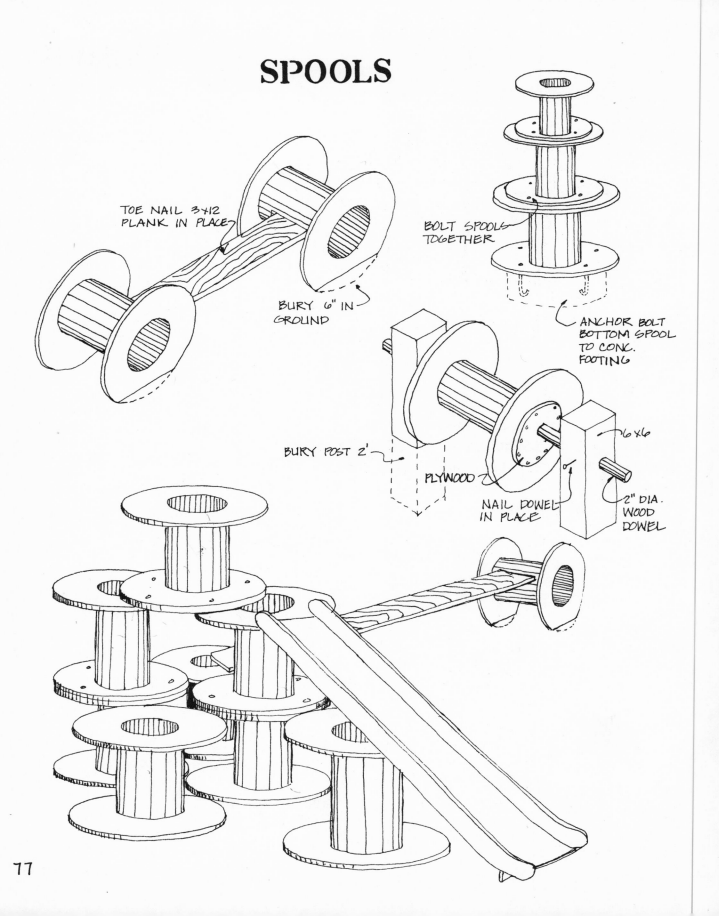

TOE NAIL 3×12
PLANK IN PLACE

BURY 6" IN
GROUND

BOLT SPOOLS
TOGETHER

ANCHOR BOLT
BOTTOM SPOOL
TO CONC.
FOOTING

BURY POST 2'

PLYWOOD

6×6

NAIL DOWEL
IN PLACE

2" DIA.
WOOD
DOWEL

DOMES

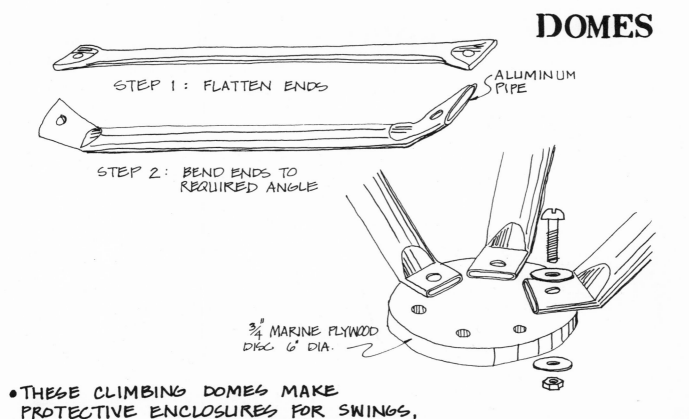

STEP 1 : FLATTEN ENDS

ALUMINUM PIPE

STEP 2 : BEND ENDS TO REQUIRED ANGLE

3/4" MARINE PLYWOOD DISC 6" DIA.

• THESE CLIMBING DOMES MAKE PROTECTIVE ENCLOSURES FOR SWINGS, LADDERS AND SLIDES AND CAN BE PLACED OVER SAND.

PIPE STRUT

PLYWOOD CONNECTOR

GEODESIC DOME

78

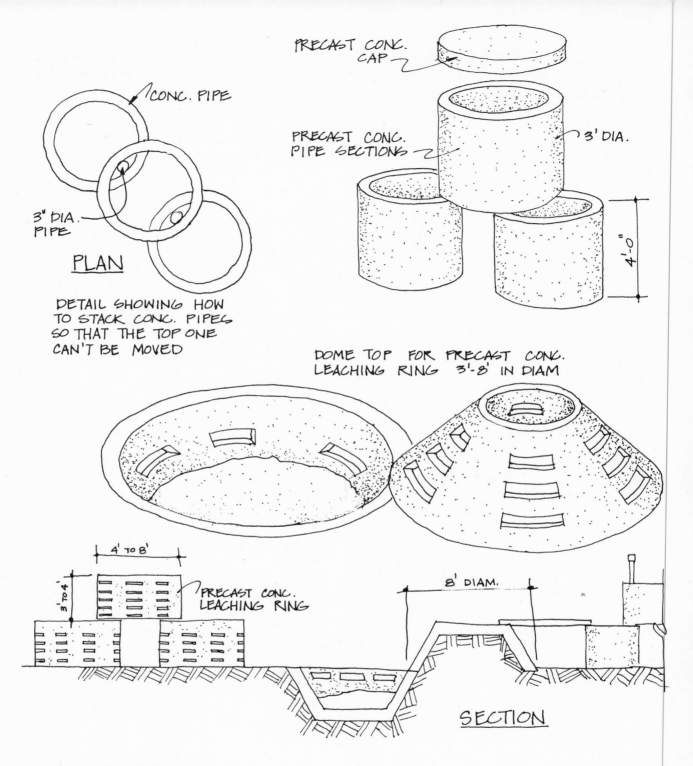

CONC. PIPE

3" DIA. PIPE

PLAN

DETAIL SHOWING HOW TO STACK CONC. PIPES SO THAT THE TOP ONE CAN'T BE MOVED

PRECAST CONC. CAP

PRECAST CONC. PIPE SECTIONS

3' DIA.

4'-0"

DOME TOP FOR PRECAST CONC. LEACHING RING 3'-8" IN DIAM

4' TO 8'

3' TO 4'

PRECAST CONC. LEACHING RING

8' DIAM.

SECTION

CONCRETE PIPE AND RINGS

79

• MASONRY STRUCTURES ARE VERY DURABLE BUT AVAILABLE ONLY IN CERTAIN PARTS OF THE COUNTRY, SOMETIMES AS SECONDS AT A MODERATE PRICE. IT IS RECOMMENDED THAT A MASONRY FILE OR STONE BE USED TO SMOOTH ROUGH CONCRETE SPOTS. THE HOLES CAN BE USED FOR SETTING PLATFORMS AND PIPES AND CLIMBING.

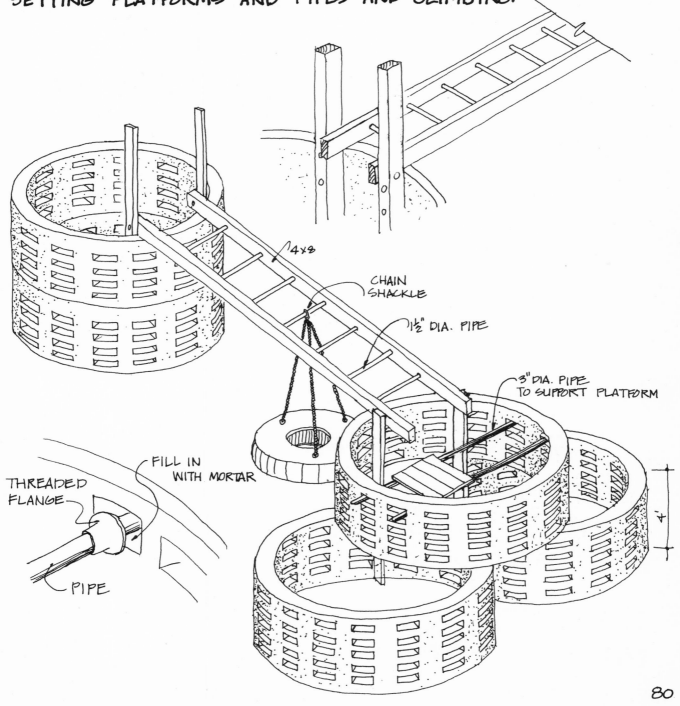

4X8

CHAIN SHACKLE

1½" DIA. PIPE

3" DIA. PIPE TO SUPPORT PLATFORM

4'

FILL IN WITH MORTAR

THREADED FLANGE

PIPE

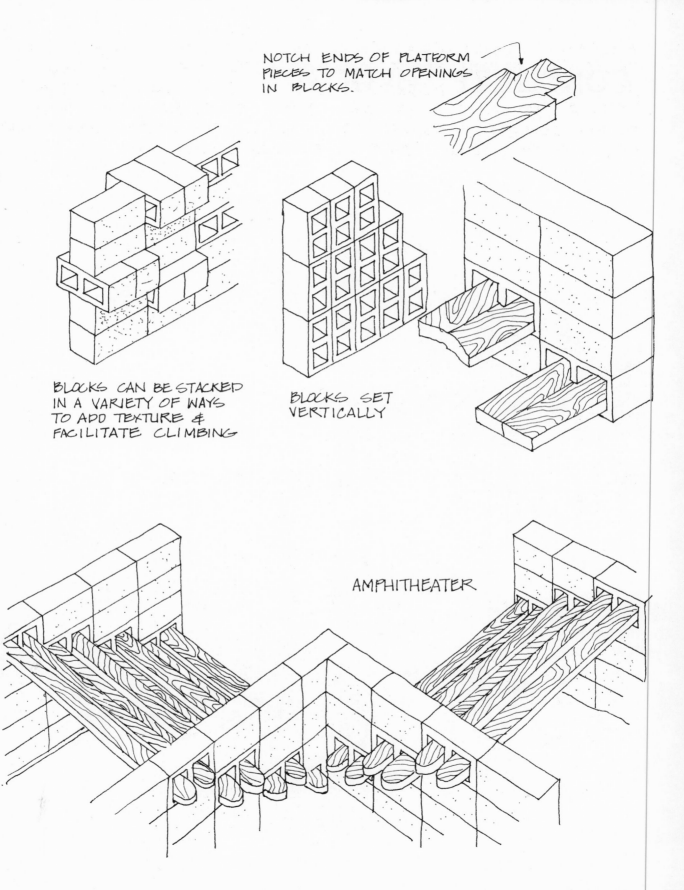

NOTCH ENDS OF PLATFORM PIECES TO MATCH OPENINGS IN BLOCKS.

BLOCKS CAN BE STACKED IN A VARIETY OF WAYS TO ADD TEXTURE & FACILITATE CLIMBING

BLOCKS SET VERTICALLY

AMPHITHEATER

CONCRETE BLOCK

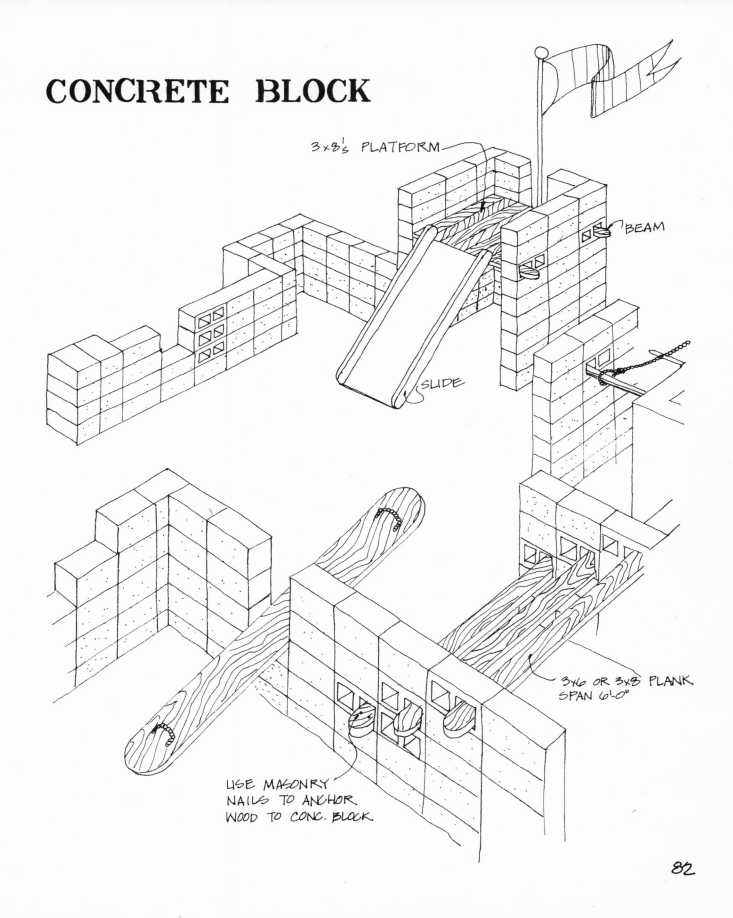

3×8's PLATFORM

BEAM

SLIDE

3×6 OR 3×8 PLANK
SPAN 6'-0"

USE MASONRY
NAILS TO ANCHOR
WOOD TO CONC. BLOCK

82

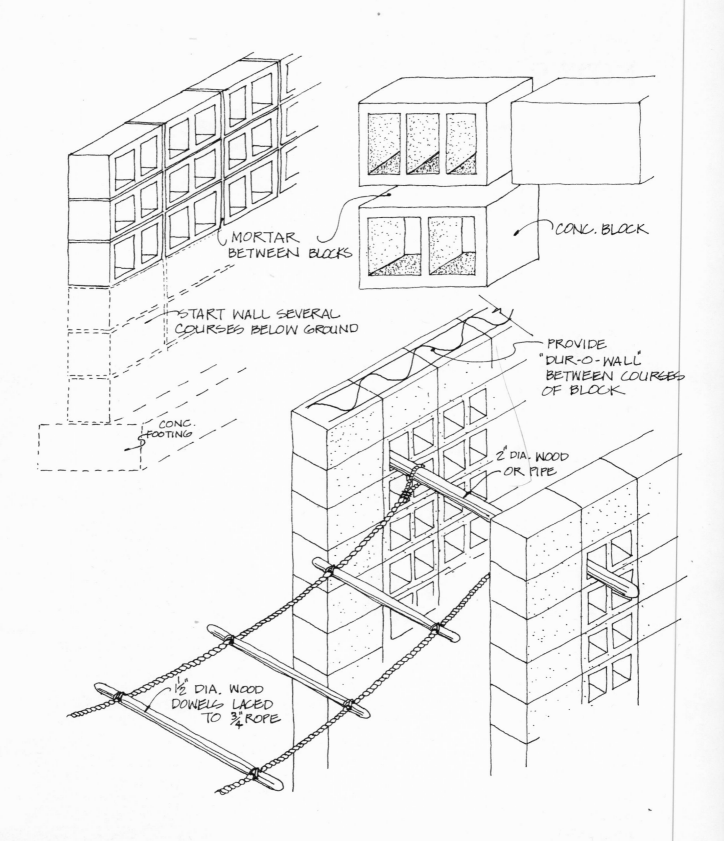

MORTAR
BETWEEN BLOCKS

CONC. BLOCK

START WALL SEVERAL
COURSES BELOW GROUND

CONC.
FOOTING

PROVIDE
"DUR-O-WALL"
BETWEEN COURSES
OF BLOCK

2" DIA. WOOD
OR PIPE

1½" DIA. WOOD
DOWELS LACED
TO ¾" ROPE

NOTES

FOOTINGS GENERALLY SHOULD BE PLACED BELOW THE FROST LINE OR SHOULD BE OF SUFFICIENT DEPTH TO PREVENT RACKING OR FAILURE. UNLESS THERE ARE PROPER FOOTINGS POLES, WHICH SUPPORT SWINGS OR LADDERS, CAN BEGIN TO SWAY AT THE TOP.

THE BEST PAVEMENTS TO USE ARE SOFT NATURAL MATERIALS THAT HAVE PLAY VALUE AND PROVIDE PROTECTION, LIKE SAND, WELL-DRAINED EARTH OR TANBARK. ONE OF THE DIFFICULTIES IN USING NATURAL MATERIALS IN HIGH DENSITY AREAS IS THE PROBLEM OF GERMS, DOGS AND MUD. THEREFORE, WHEN IT IS NOT FEASIBLE TO USE NATURAL MATERIALS, I WOULD RECOMMEND SOME OF THE COMMERCIALLY MANUFACTURED RESILIENT PAVEMENTS SUCH AS RUBBER MATS OR RESILIENT ASPHALT PAVEMENT

ACCESSORIES

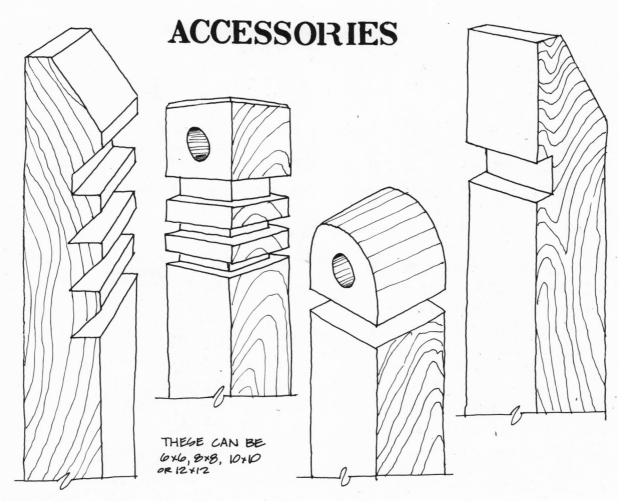

THESE CAN BE
6x6, 8x8, 10x10
OR 12x12

- <u>ACCESSORIES</u>
  THE FOLLOWING COMPONENTS
  ARE ACCESSORIES THAT
  SUPPORT PLAYGROUND
  ACTIVITIES SUCH AS SWINGS,
  SLIDES, BIKE RACKS, ETC.

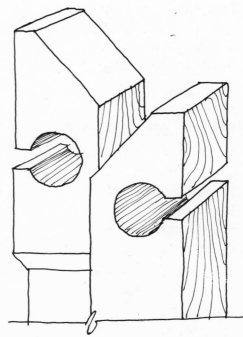

COLUMN
CAPITALS

CABLE AND PIPE SLIDE

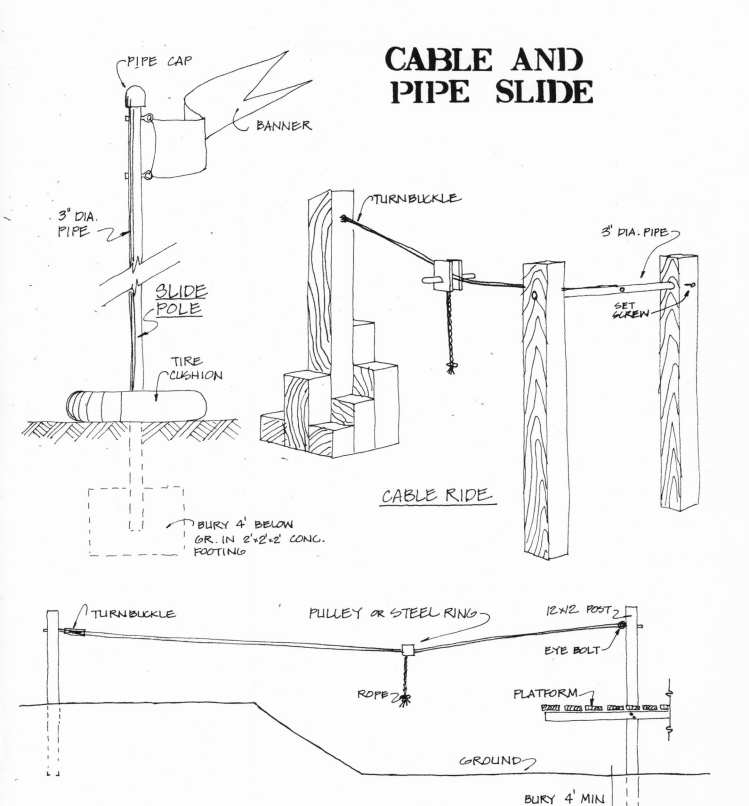

PIPE CAP

BANNER

3" DIA. PIPE

SLIDE POLE

TIRE CUSHION

BURY 4' BELOW GR. IN 2'x2'x2' CONC. FOOTING

TURNBUCKLE

3" DIA. PIPE

SET SCREW

CABLE RIDE

TURNBUCKLE

PULLEY OR STEEL RING

12x12 POST

EYE BOLT

ROPE

PLATFORM

GROUND

BURY 4' MIN

86

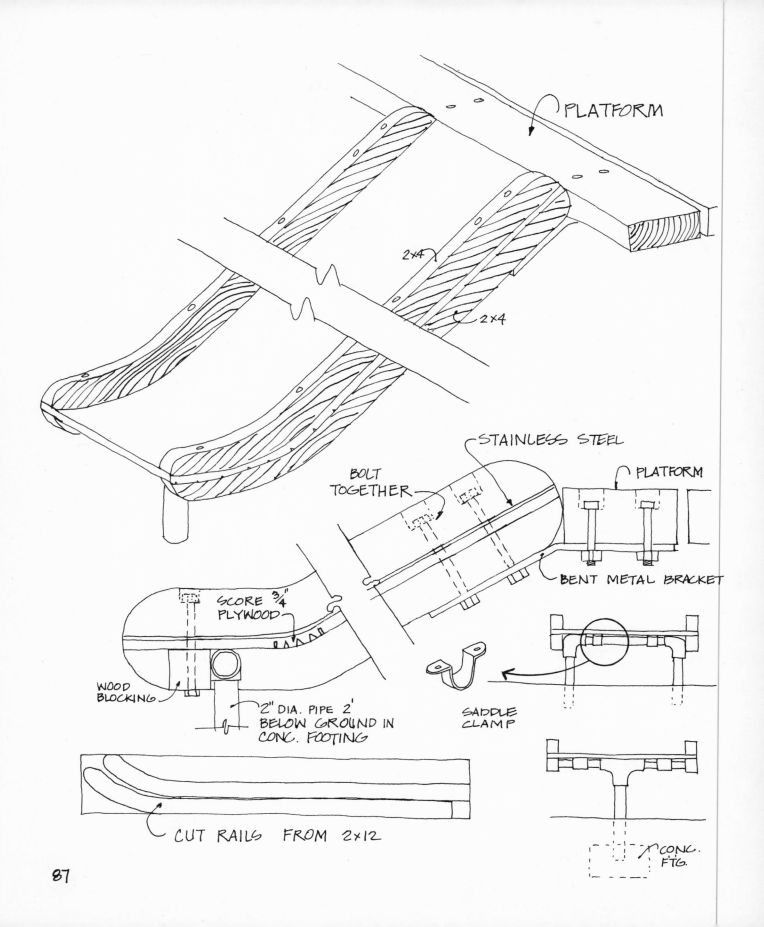

PLATFORM

2×4

2×4

STAINLESS STEEL

BOLT TOGETHER

PLATFORM

BENT METAL BRACKET

SCORE 3/4" PLYWOOD

WOOD BLOCKING

2" DIA. PIPE 2' BELOW GROUND IN CONC. FOOTING

SADDLE CLAMP

CUT RAILS FROM 2×12

CONC. FTG.

87

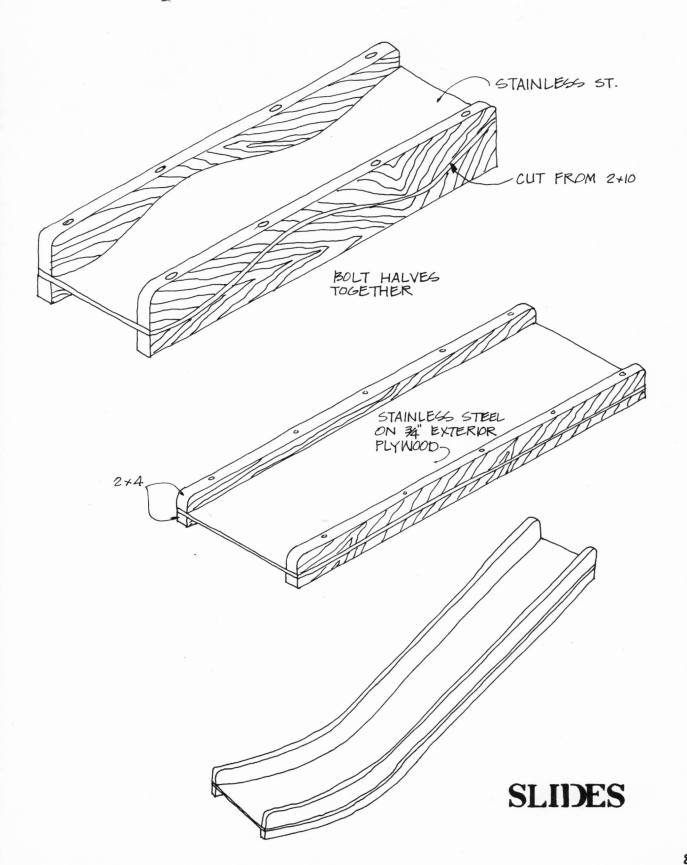

STAINLESS ST.

CUT FROM 2×10

BOLT HALVES
TOGETHER

STAINLESS STEEL
ON 3/4" EXTERIOR
PLYWOOD

2×4

SLIDES

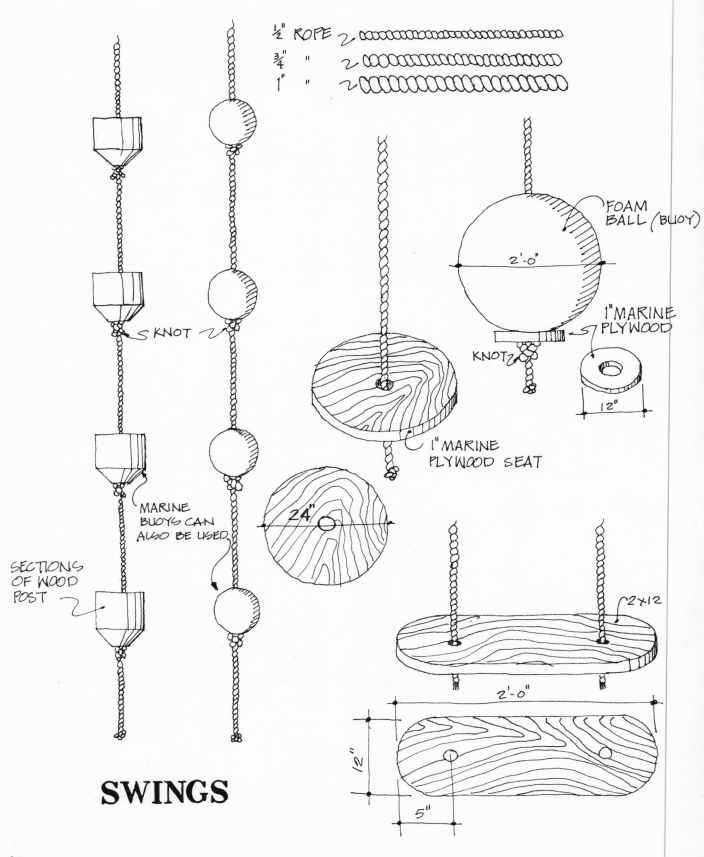

½" ROPE 2

¾" " 2

1" " 2

KNOT

FOAM BALL (BUOY)

2'-0"

1" MARINE PLYWOOD

KNOT

12"

1" MARINE PLYWOOD SEAT

24"

MARINE BUOYS CAN ALSO BE USED

SECTIONS OF WOOD POST

2×12

2'-0"

12"

5"

SWINGS

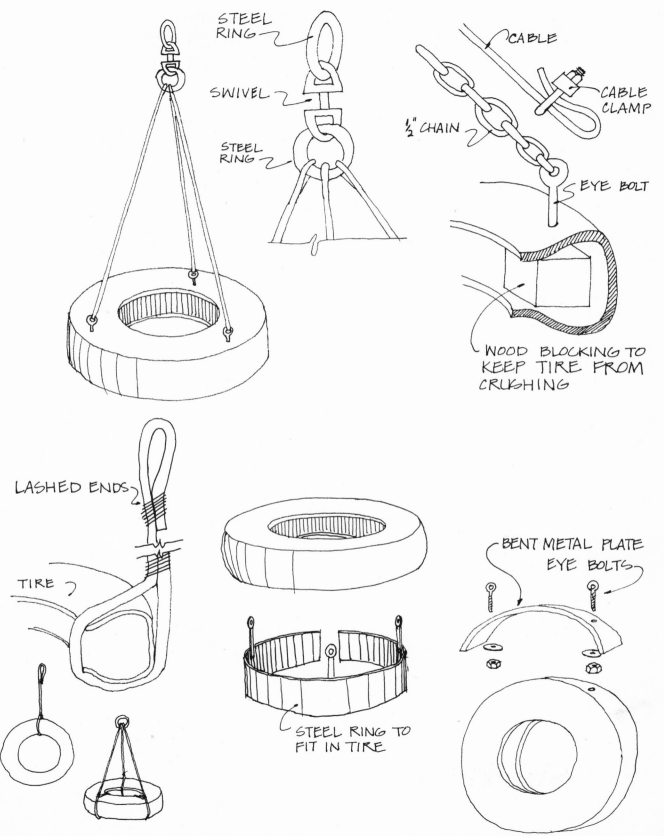

STEEL RING

SWIVEL

STEEL RING

CABLE

CABLE CLAMP

½" CHAIN

EYE BOLT

WOOD BLOCKING TO KEEP TIRE FROM CRUSHING

LASHED ENDS

TIRE

STEEL RING TO FIT IN TIRE

BENT METAL PLATE EYE BOLTS

90

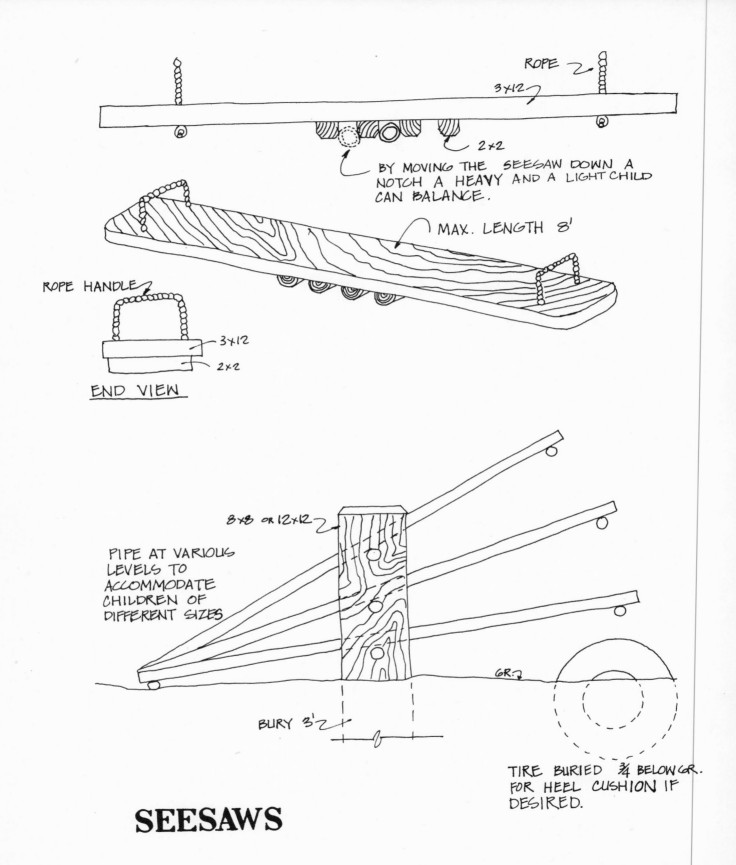

ROPE

3×12

2×2

BY MOVING THE SEESAW DOWN A
NOTCH A HEAVY AND A LIGHT CHILD
CAN BALANCE.

MAX. LENGTH 8'

ROPE HANDLE

3×12

2×2

END VIEW

8×8 or 12×12

PIPE AT VARIOUS
LEVELS TO
ACCOMMODATE
CHILDREN OF
DIFFERENT SIZES

GR.

BURY 3'

TIRE BURIED ¾ BELOW GR.
FOR HEEL CUSHION IF
DESIRED.

SEESAWS

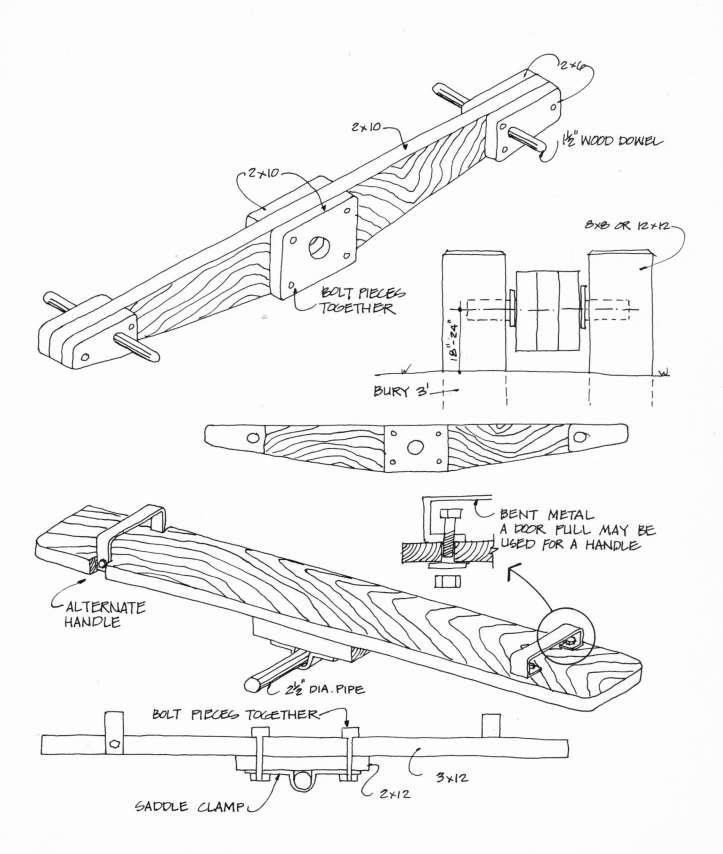

2×6

2×10

1½" WOOD DOWEL

2×10

BOLT PIECES TOGETHER

8×8 OR 12×12

18"-24"

BURY 3'

BENT METAL
A DOOR PULL MAY BE
USED FOR A HANDLE

ALTERNATE
HANDLE

2½" DIA. PIPE

BOLT PIECES TOGETHER

SADDLE CLAMP

2×12

3×12

92

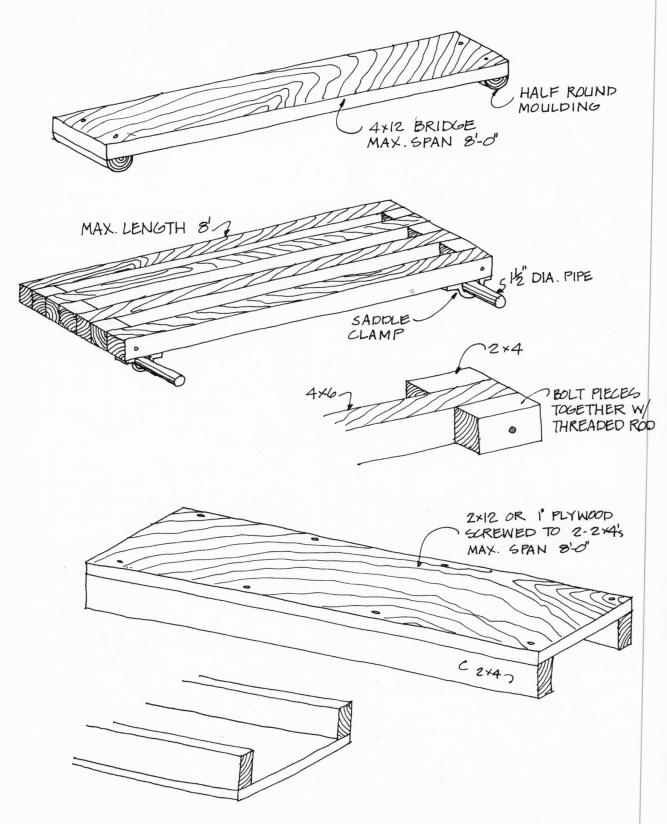

HALF ROUND
MOULDING

4×12 BRIDGE
MAX. SPAN 8'-0"

MAX. LENGTH 8'

1½" DIA. PIPE

SADDLE
CLAMP

2×4

4×6

BOLT PIECES
TOGETHER W/
THREADED ROD

2×12 OR 1" PLYWOOD
SCREWED TO 2-2×4's
MAX. SPAN 8'-0"

(2×4)

93

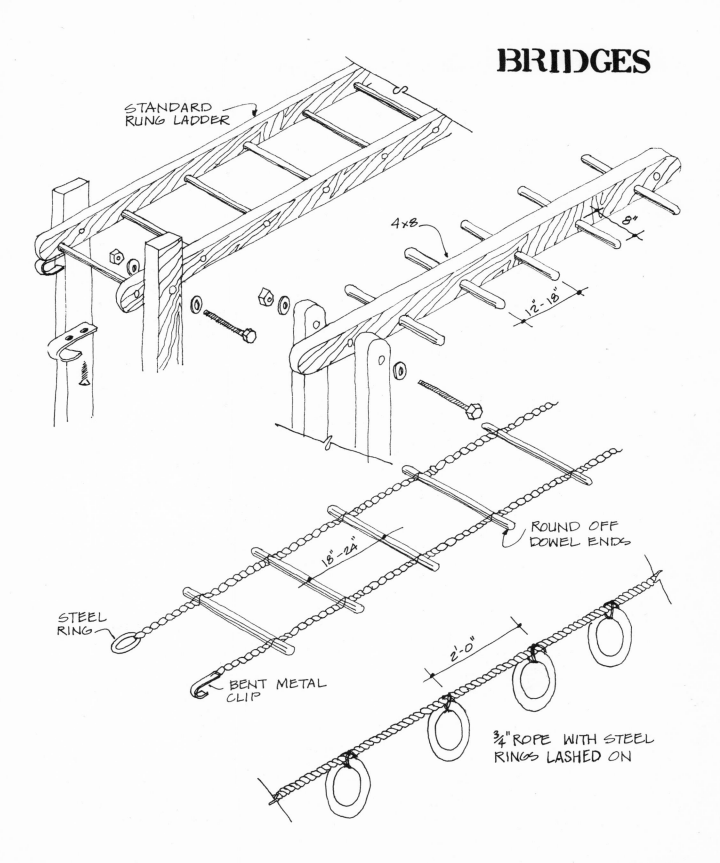

BRIDGES

STANDARD RUNG LADDER

4×8

8"

12"-18"

ROUND OFF DOWEL ENDS

STEEL RING

18"-24"

BENT METAL CLIP

2'-0"

¾" ROPE WITH STEEL RINGS LASHED ON

94

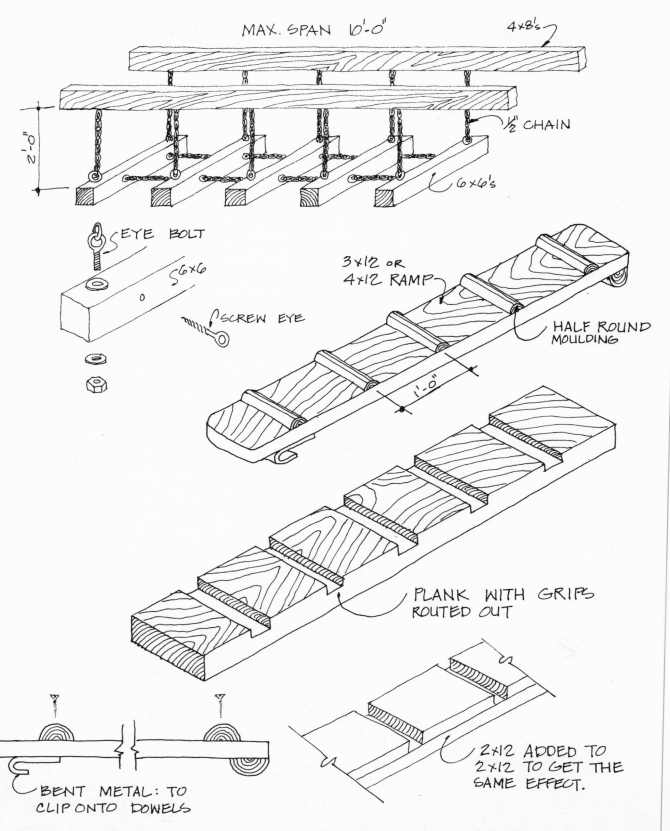

MAX. SPAN 10'-0"

4×8's

½" CHAIN

2'-0"

6×6's

EYE BOLT

6×6

SCREW EYE

3×12 OR
4×12 RAMP

HALF ROUND
MOULDING

1'-0"

PLANK WITH GRIPS
ROUTED OUT

BENT METAL: TO
CLIP ONTO DOWELS

2×12 ADDED TO
2×12 TO GET THE
SAME EFFECT.

NOTES

WHEN USING PIPE, IT IS ADVISABLE TO PLUG UP THE ENDS OF THE PIPE TO PREVENT FINGERS GETTING STUCK. WHEN PIPES AND DOWELS ARE USED, MAKE CERTAIN THEY ARE WIDE ENOUGH NOT TO POKE OUT A CHILD'S EYE — A MINIMUM OF 1½" IN DIAMETER IS RECOMMENDED.

WHEN USING CABLE, COVER IT WITH GARDEN HOSE OR USE VINYL-COATED CABLE. NEVER USE A CABLE SO THIN THAT A CHILD CANNOT GRASP IT EASILY. A MINIMUM OF 1½" IS RECOMMENDED.

NEVER FASTEN (NAIL OR SCREW) INTO THE END GRAIN OF WOOD AS IT HAS NO STRUCTURAL CAPABILITY IN THAT DIRECTION.

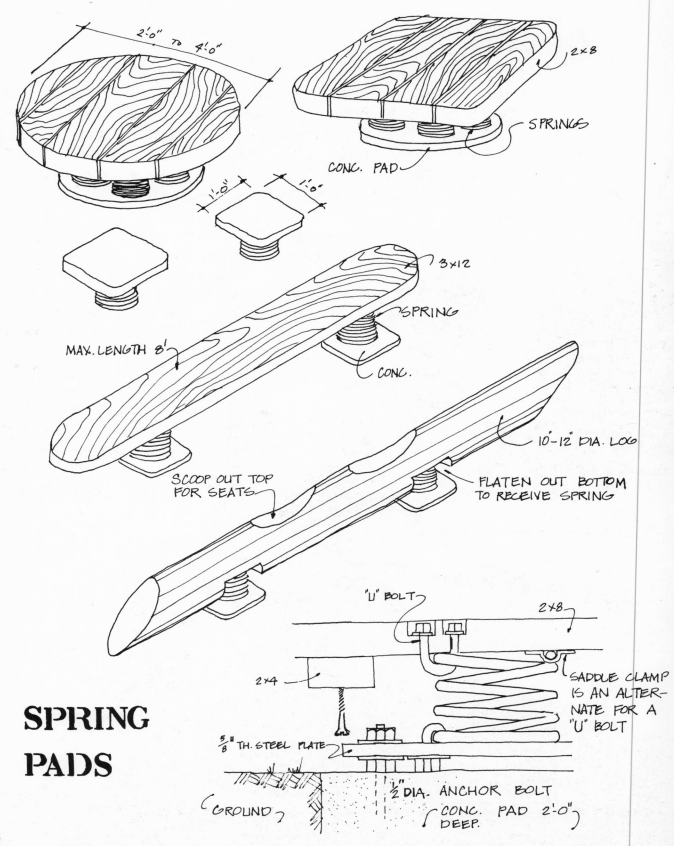

2'-0" TO 4'-0"

2×8

SPRINGS

CONC. PAD

1'-0" 1'-0"

3×12

SPRING

MAX. LENGTH 8'

CONC.

10'-12" DIA. LOG

SCOOP OUT TOP FOR SEATS.

FLATEN OUT BOTTOM TO RECEIVE SPRING

"U" BOLT

2×8

2×4

SADDLE CLAMP IS AN ALTERNATE FOR A "U" BOLT

⅝" TH. STEEL PLATE

SPRING PADS

½" DIA. ANCHOR BOLT

CONC. PAD 2'-0" DEEP.

GROUND

97

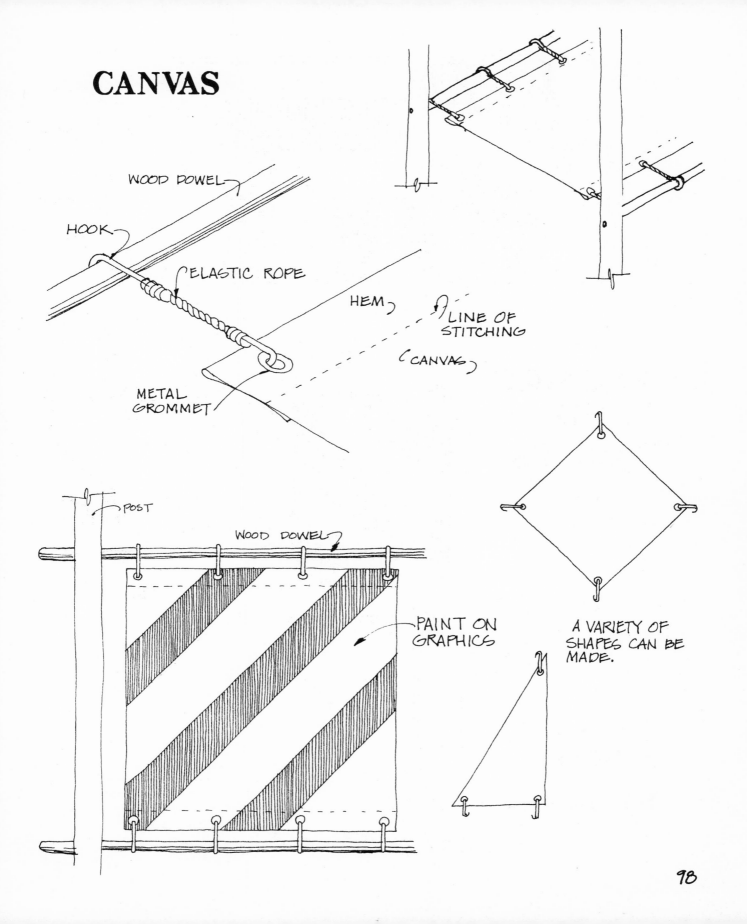

CANVAS

WOOD DOWEL

HOOK

ELASTIC ROPE

HEM

LINE OF STITCHING

(CANVAS)

METAL GROMMET

POST

WOOD DOWEL

PAINT ON GRAPHICS

A VARIETY OF SHAPES CAN BE MADE.

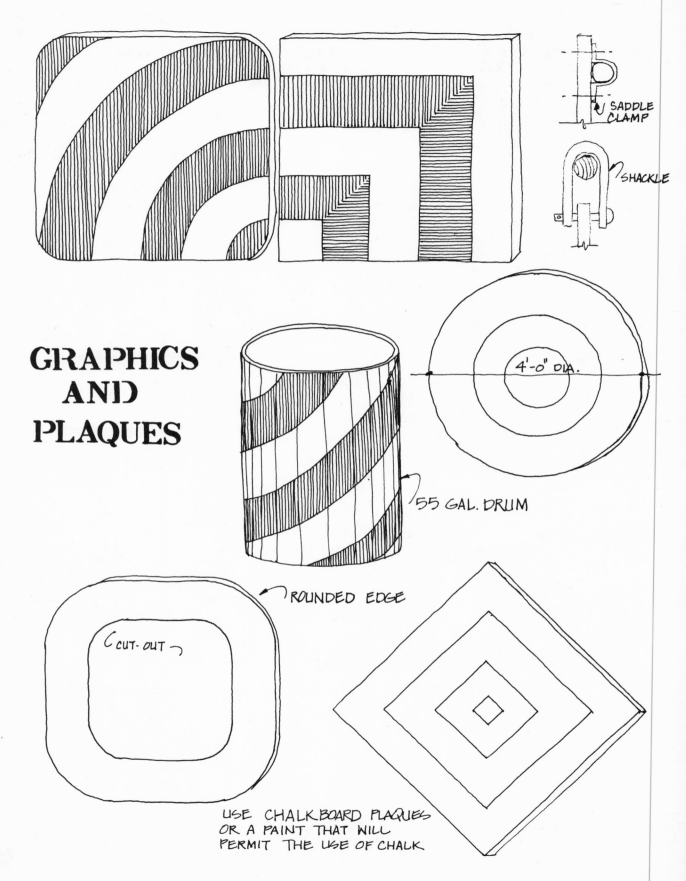

GRAPHICS AND PLAQUES

SADDLE CLAMP

SHACKLE

4'-0" DIA.

55 GAL. DRUM

ROUNDED EDGE

CUT-OUT

USE CHALKBOARD PLAQUES
OR A PAINT THAT WILL
PERMIT THE USE OF CHALK

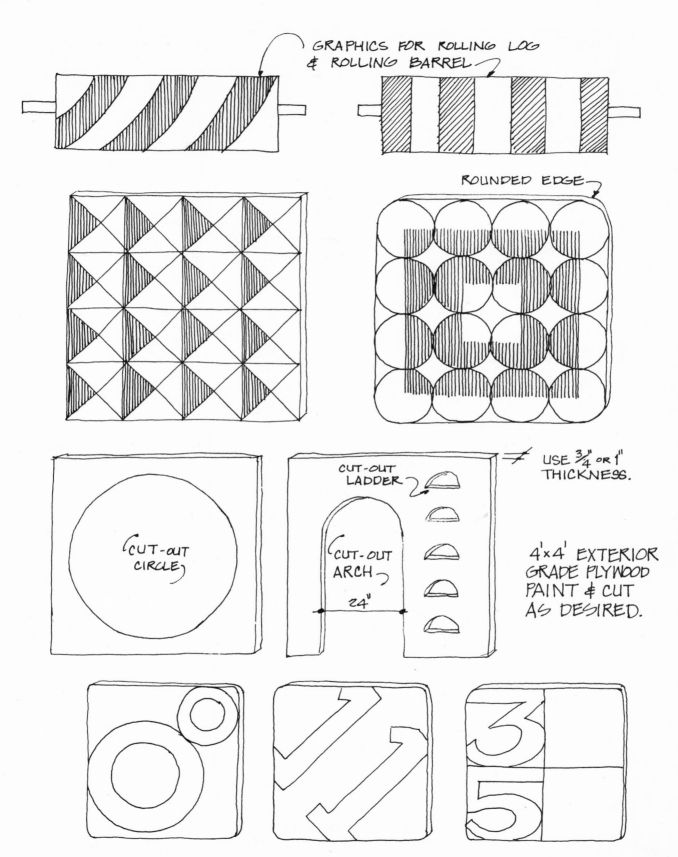

GRAPHICS FOR ROLLING LOG & ROLLING BARREL

ROUNDED EDGE

CUT-OUT CIRCLE

CUT-OUT LADDER

CUT-OUT ARCH

24"

USE 3/4" OR 1" THICKNESS.

4'x4' EXTERIOR GRADE PLYWOOD PAINT & CUT AS DESIRED.

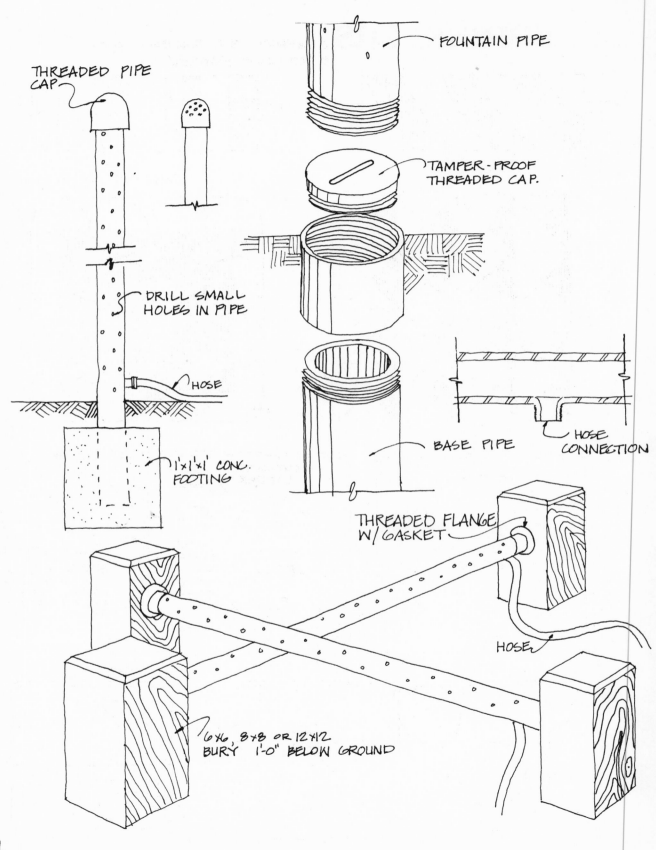

THREADED PIPE CAP

FOUNTAIN PIPE

TAMPER-PROOF THREADED CAP.

DRILL SMALL HOLES IN PIPE

HOSE

1'x1'x1' CONC. FOOTING

BASE PIPE

HOSE CONNECTION

THREADED FLANGE W/ GASKET

HOSE

6x6, 8x8 or 12x12 BURY 1'-0" BELOW GROUND

SPRINKLERS

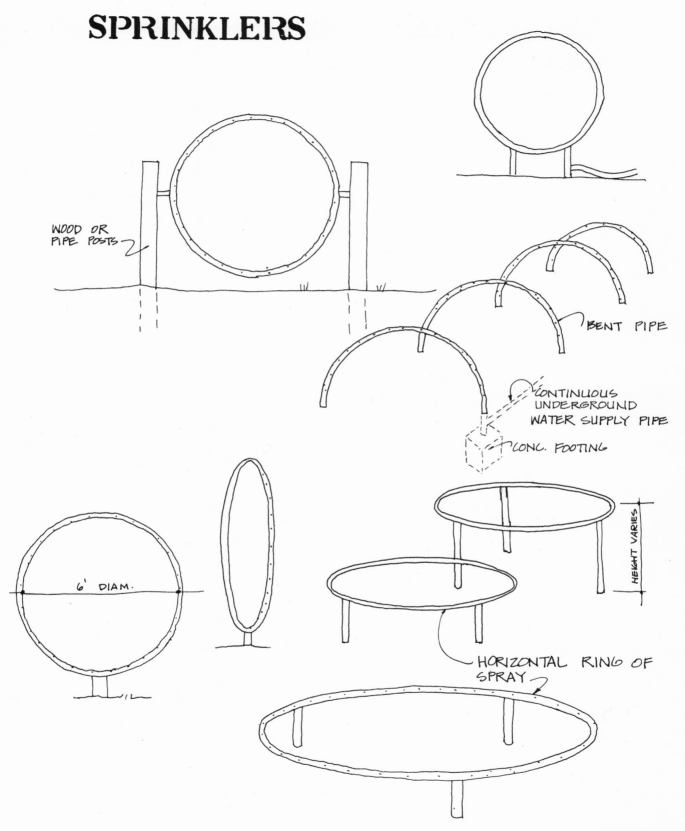

WOOD OR PIPE POSTS

BENT PIPE

CONTINUOUS UNDERGROUND WATER SUPPLY PIPE

CONC. FOOTING

6' DIAM.

HEIGHT VARIES

HORIZONTAL RING OF SPRAY

FOUNTAINS

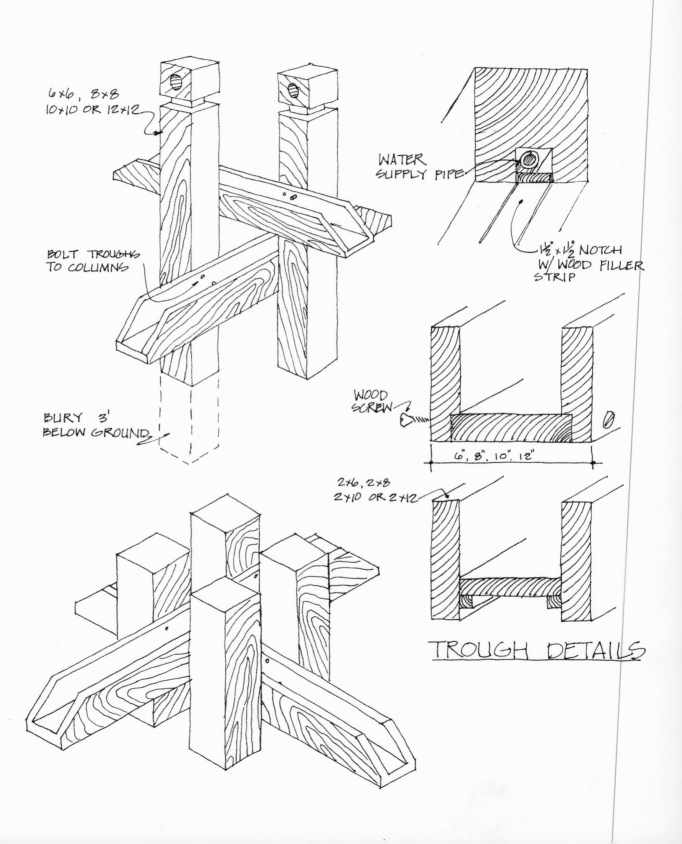

6×6, 8×8
10×10 OR 12×12

BOLT TROUGHS
TO COLUMNS

BURY 3'
BELOW GROUND

WATER
SUPPLY PIPE

$1\frac{1}{2}$" × $1\frac{1}{2}$" NOTCH
W/ WOOD FILLER
STRIP

WOOD
SCREW

6", 8", 10", 12"

2×6, 2×8
2×10 OR 2×12

TROUGH DETAILS

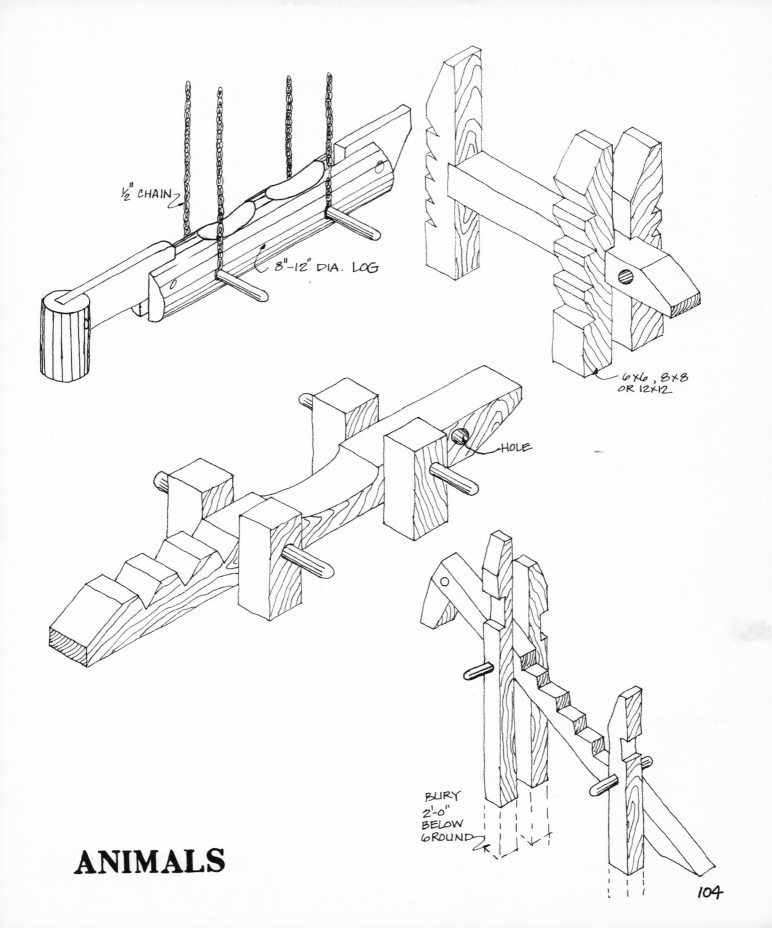

½" CHAIN

8"-12" DIA. LOG

6×6 , 8×8
OR 12×12

HOLE

BURY
2'-0"
BELOW
GROUND

ANIMALS

104

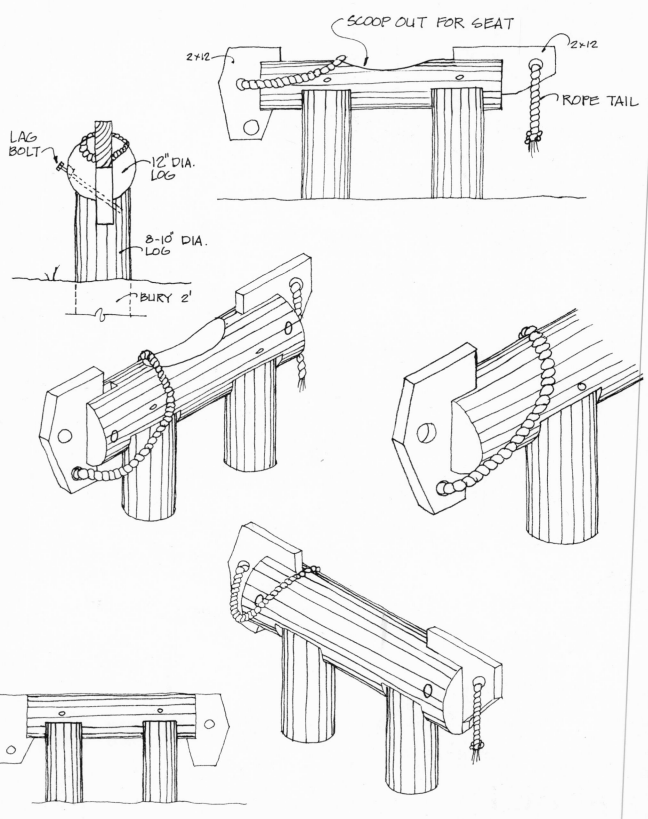

SCOOP OUT FOR SEAT

2×12

2×12

ROPE TAIL

LAG
BOLT

12" DIA.
LOG

8-10" DIA.
LOG

BURY 2'

105

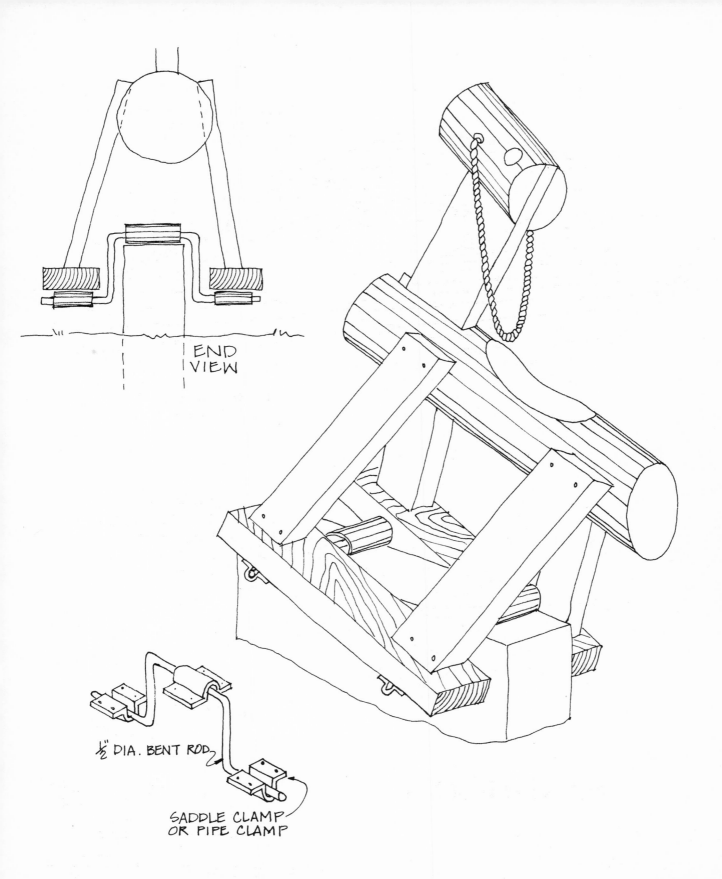

END
VIEW

½ DIA. BENT ROD

SADDLE CLAMP
OR PIPE CLAMP

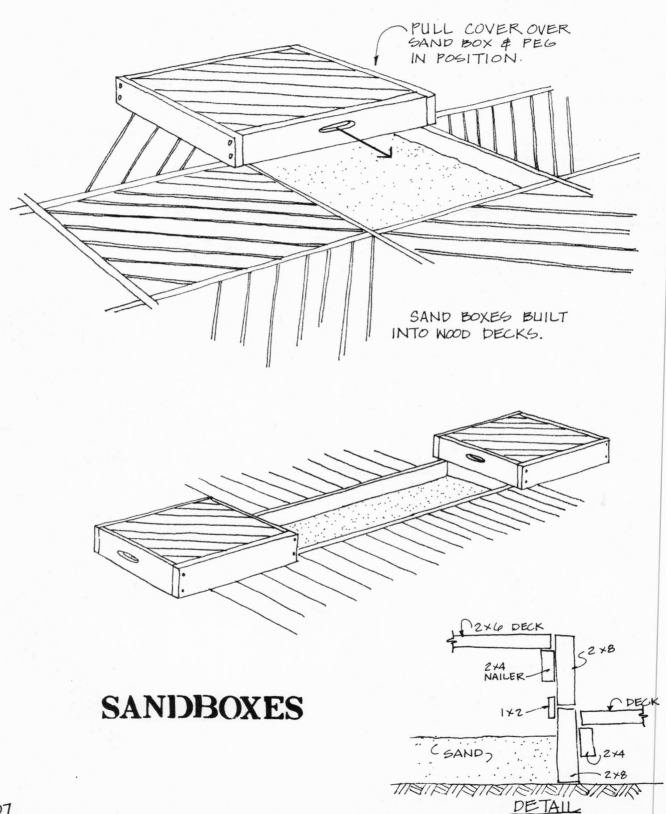

PULL COVER OVER
SAND BOX & PEG
IN POSITION.

SAND BOXES BUILT
INTO WOOD DECKS.

2×6 DECK

2×4
NAILER

2×8

1×2

DECK

SAND

2×4

2×8

DETAIL

SANDBOXES

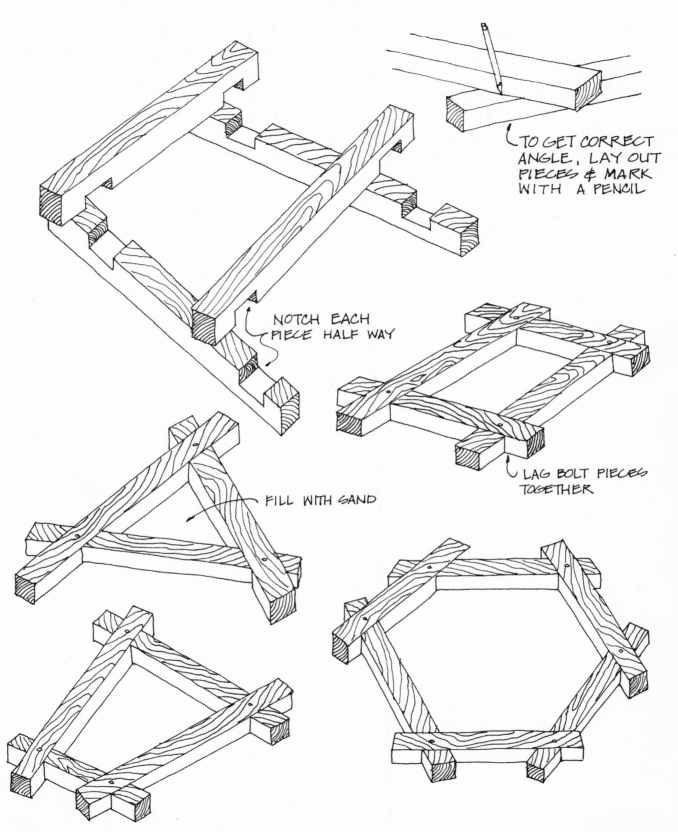

TO GET CORRECT ANGLE, LAY OUT PIECES & MARK WITH A PENCIL

NOTCH EACH PIECE HALF WAY

LAG BOLT PIECES TOGETHER

FILL WITH SAND

• SAND, LIKE WATER, IS A RESPONSIVE ELEMENT WHICH ALLOWS A WIDE RANGE OF MANIPULATION AND SHOULD PERVADE THE PLAYGROUND RATHER THAN BEING CONTAINED IN A CONVENTIONAL BOX. SAND ALSO ACTS AS A BUFFER AND SHOULD BE PLACED AT THE BOTTOM OF SLIDES OR AT THE BASE OF SPRING PADS OR OTHER POINTS OF INTENSE ACTIVITY.

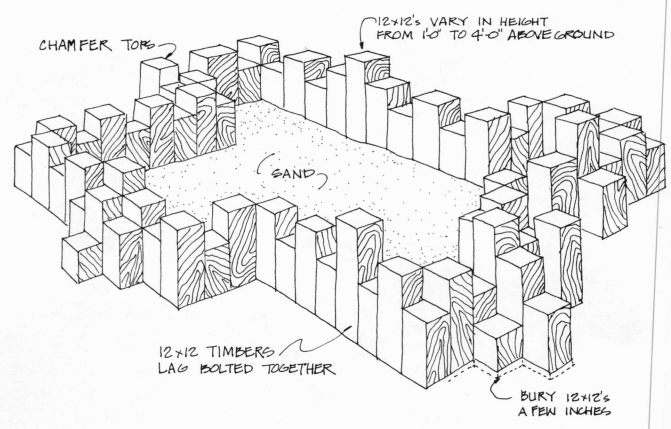

CHAMFER TOPS

12×12's VARY IN HEIGHT FROM 1'-0" TO 4'-0" ABOVEGROUND

SAND

12×12 TIMBERS LAG BOLTED TOGETHER

BURY 12×12's A FEW INCHES

THERE ARE NO LIMITS TO THE SIZE OR SHAPE OF THIS TYPE SAND BOX.

NOTES

WHEN USING ROPE OR CABLE, ALWAYS ANTICIPATE THAT A CERTAIN AMOUNT OF STRETCHING WILL OCCUR. PROVIDE FOR THIS BY CONSTANT TIGHTENING THROUGH THE USE OF TURNBUCKLES, EYE BOLTS, ETC.

MAKE SURE THAT ALL ELEMENTS IN THE PLAYGROUND THAT ARE SUPPOSED TO BE FIXED ARE RIGID. CHILDREN TEND TO EXPERIMENT WITH ANYTHING THAT MOVES AT ALL, AND CONSTANT JIGGLING OR SWINGING CAN BE DANGEROUS.

PLANTERS

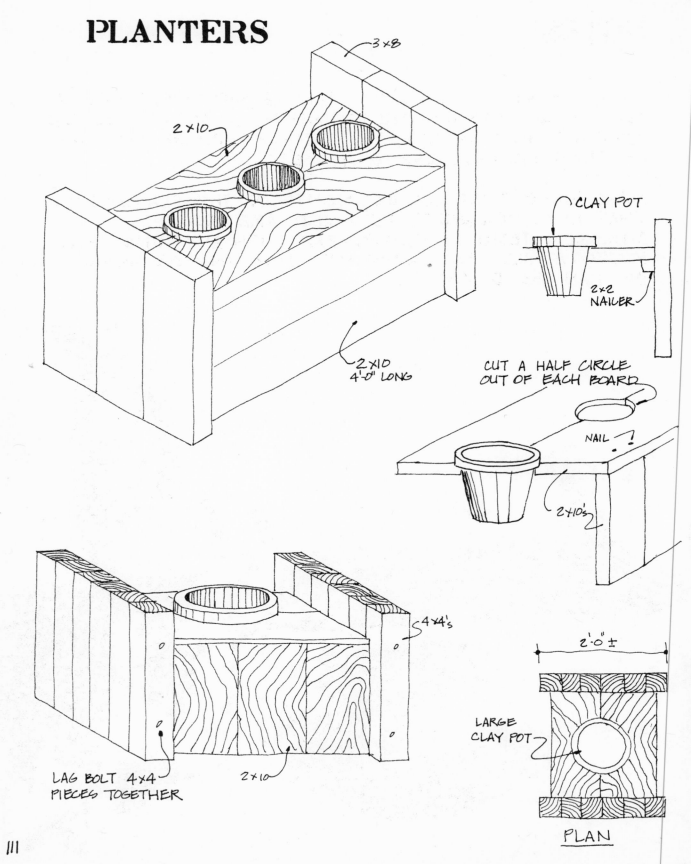

3×8

2×10

CLAY POT

2×10
4'-0" LONG

2×2
NAILER

CUT A HALF CIRCLE
OUT OF EACH BOARD

NAIL

2×10's

4×4's

LAG BOLT 4×4
PIECES TOGETHER

2×10

2'-0" ±

LARGE
CLAY POT

PLAN

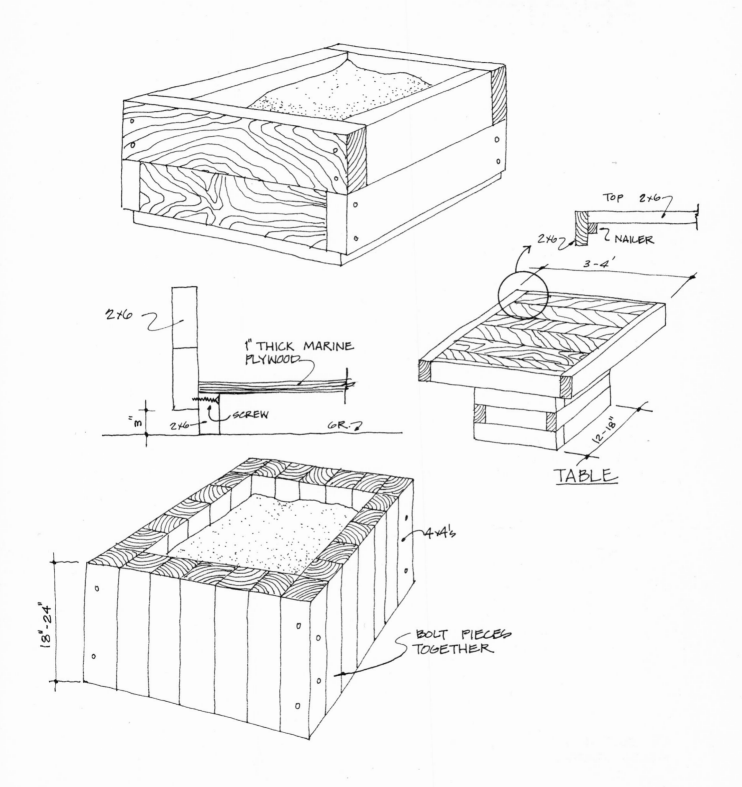

TOP 2×6

2×6

NAILER

3 - 4'

2×6

1" THICK MARINE PLYWOOD

SCREW

2×6

GR.

12-18"

TABLE

4×4's

18"-24"

BOLT PIECES
TOGETHER

BENCHES

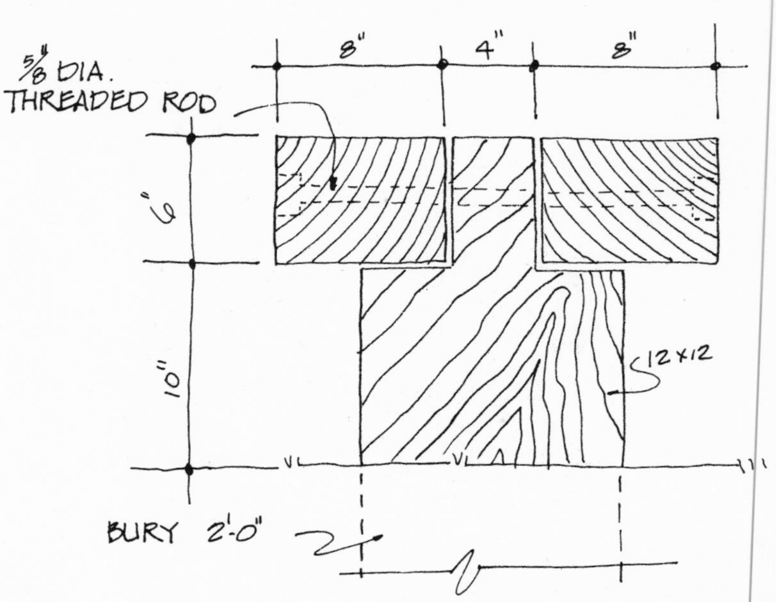

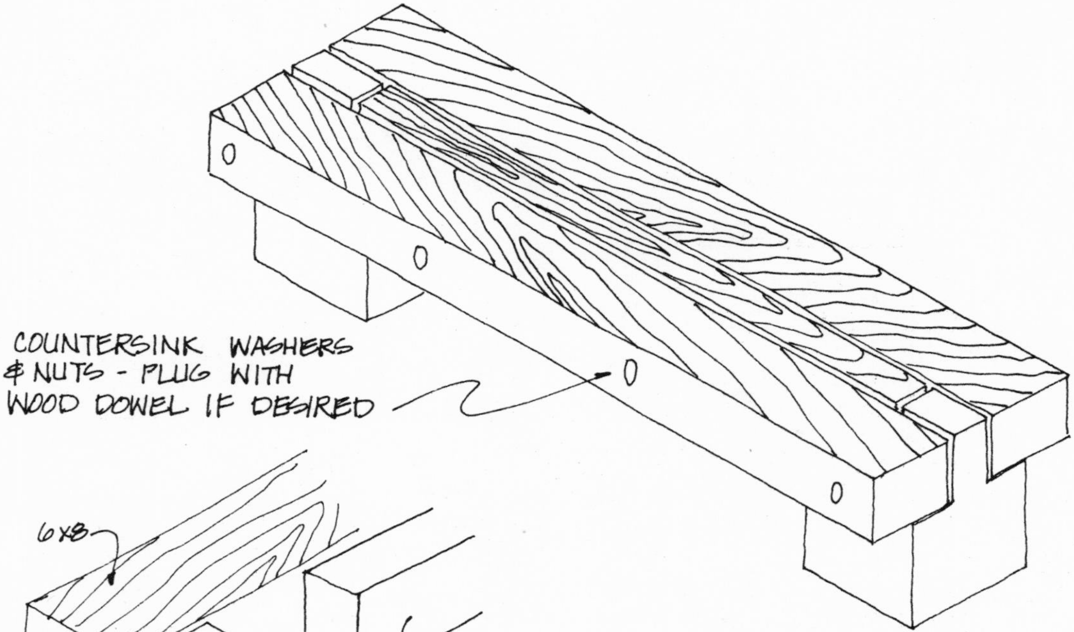

5/8" DIA. THREADED ROD

8" | 4" | 8"

6"

10"

12×12

BURY 2'-0"

COUNTERSINK WASHERS
& NUTS - PLUG WITH
WOOD DOWEL IF DESIRED

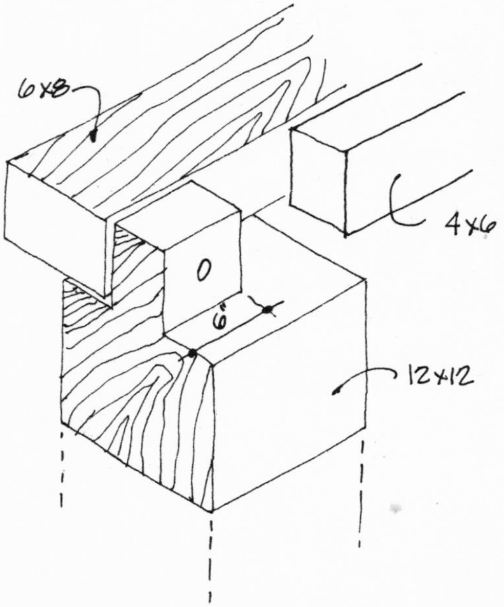

6×8

4×6

6"

12×12

THIS BENCH CAN BE
6' TO 12' LONG.

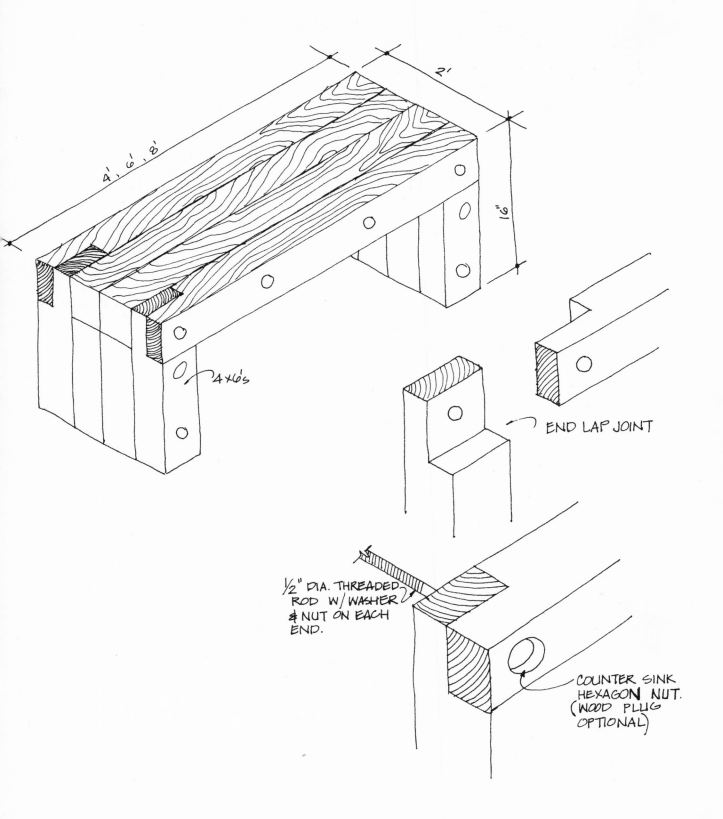

2'

6"

4', 6', 8'

4 x 6's

END LAP JOINT

½" DIA. THREADED
ROD W/ WASHER
& NUT ON EACH
END.

COUNTER SINK
HEXAGON NUT.
(WOOD PLUG
OPTIONAL)

114

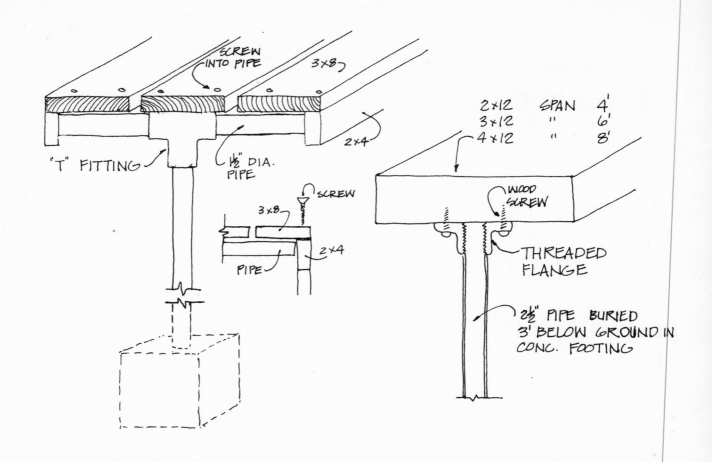

SCREW INTO PIPE

3×8

"T" FITTING

1½" DIA. PIPE

2×4

SCREW

3×8

2×4

PIPE

2×12   SPAN   4'
3×12   "   6'
4×12   "   8'

WOOD SCREW

THREADED FLANGE

2½" PIPE BURIED 3' BELOW GROUND IN CONC. FOOTING

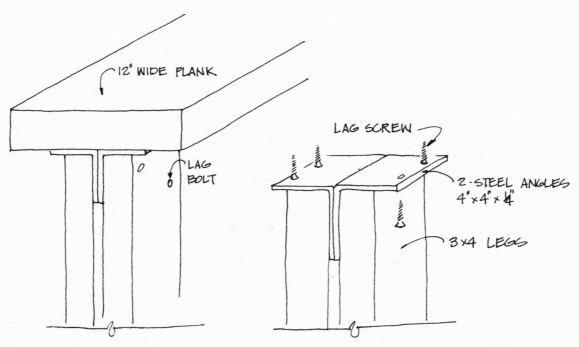

12" WIDE PLANK

LAG BOLT

LAG SCREW

2-STEEL ANGLES 4"×4"×¼"

3×4 LEGS

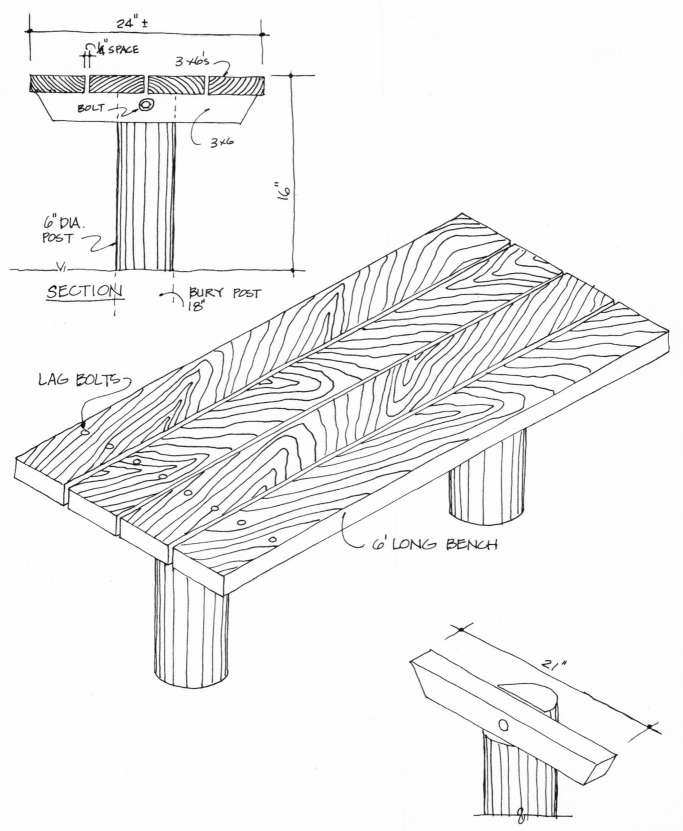

24" ±

1/4" SPACE

3 ×6's

BOLT

3×6

16"

6" DIA. POST

SECTION

BURY POST 18"

LAG BOLTS

6' LONG BENCH

21"

116

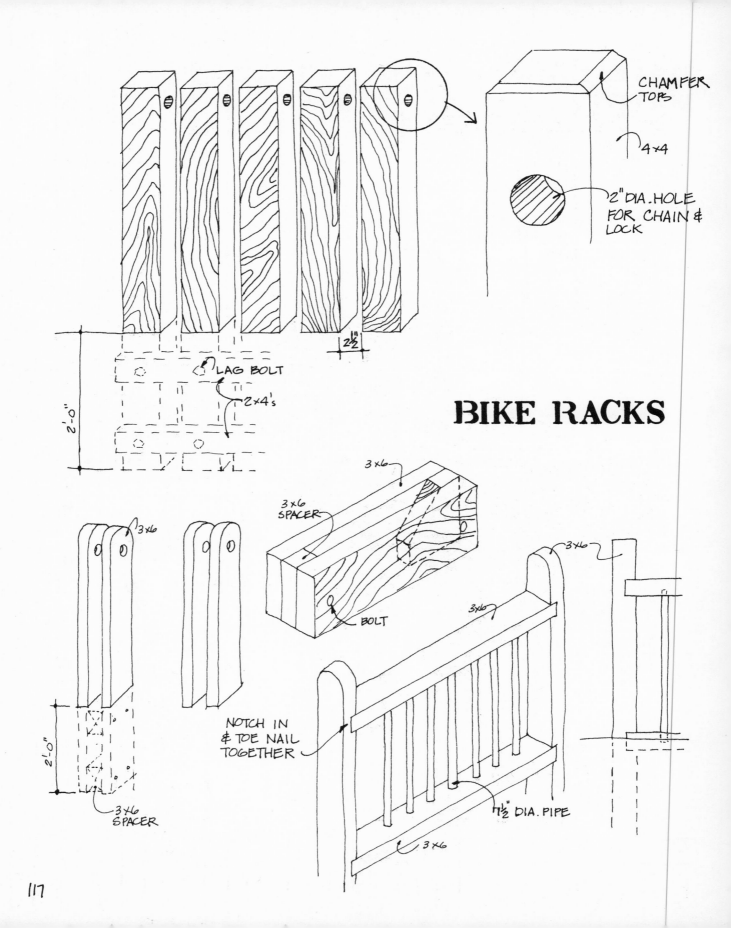

CHAMFER TOPS

4×4

2" DIA. HOLE FOR CHAIN & LOCK

2½"

LAG BOLT

2×4's

2'-0"

BIKE RACKS

3×6

3×6 SPACER

3×6

BOLT

3×6

3×6

3×6

NOTCH IN & TOE NAIL TOGETHER

7½" DIA. PIPE

3×6

3×6 SPACER

2'-0"

MATERIALS MATRIX

	Hardware Store	Lumber Yard	Chemical Co.	Garden Center	Service Station	Junk Yard	Marine Supply	Building Supply	Mail Order (Sears)	Plumbing Supply	Wire & Chain Co.	Telephone Co.	Awning Maker	Lighting/Utility Co.	Railroad	General Contractor	Auto Supply Co.	Sheet Metal Works	Demolished Bldg.
CHAIN	●						●				●								
FASTENERS: BOLTS, NAILS, SCREWS, ETC.	●	●					●	●	●										
55 GAL. DRUMS			●		●	●													
SPRINGS	●				●	●											●		
STAINLESS STEEL								●										●	
CANVAS							●						●						
PIPE	●						●			●									
HOSE	●			●						●									
ROPE	●						●												
CABLE & FASTENERS	●						●				●								
STEEL ANGLES/CHANNELS							●	●								●		●	
NETS	●						●	●											
CONCRETE BLOCK		●						●											●
LEACHING RINGS								●		●						●			
WOOD / LUMBER		●																	●
SPOOLS												●		●		●			
TELEPHONE POLES		●						●				●		●					
TIMBERS / R.R. TIES		●													●				●
FENCE	●			●				●											●
LADDERS	●	●						●											
DOWELS		●																	
WATER TANKS																			●
TIRES						●											●		
SCAFFOLDING								●								●			

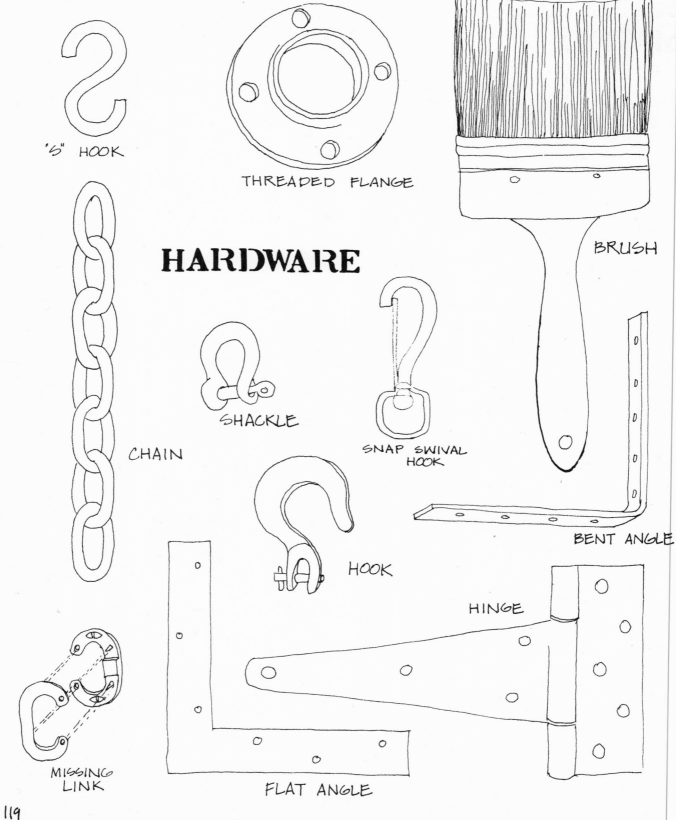

"S" HOOK

THREADED FLANGE

BRUSH

HARDWARE

CHAIN

SHACKLE

SNAP SWIVAL
HOOK

HOOK

BENT ANGLE

HINGE

MISSING
LINK

FLAT ANGLE

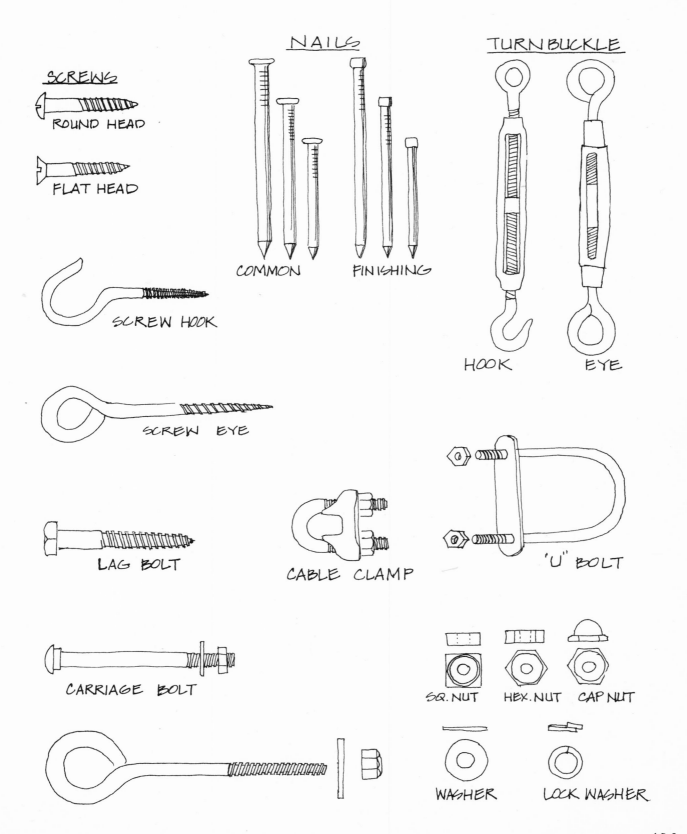

SCREWS

ROUND HEAD

FLAT HEAD

SCREW HOOK

SCREW EYE

LAG BOLT

CARRIAGE BOLT

NAILS

COMMON

FINISHING

CABLE CLAMP

TURNBUCKLE

HOOK

EYE

"U" BOLT

SQ. NUT   HEX. NUT   CAP NUT

WASHER   LOCK WASHER

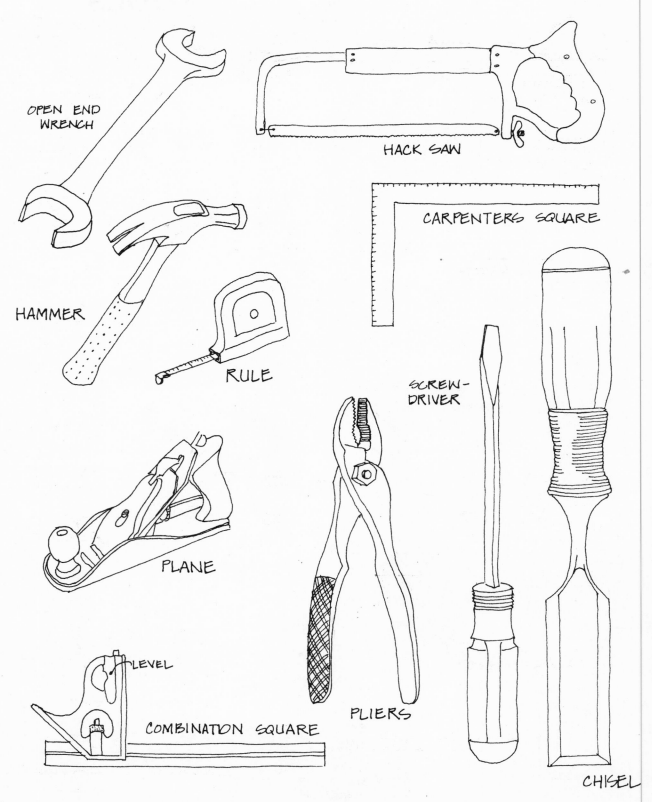

OPEN END WRENCH

HACK SAW

CARPENTERS SQUARE

HAMMER

RULE

SCREW-DRIVER

PLANE

LEVEL

COMBINATON SQUARE

PLIERS

CHISEL

TOOLS

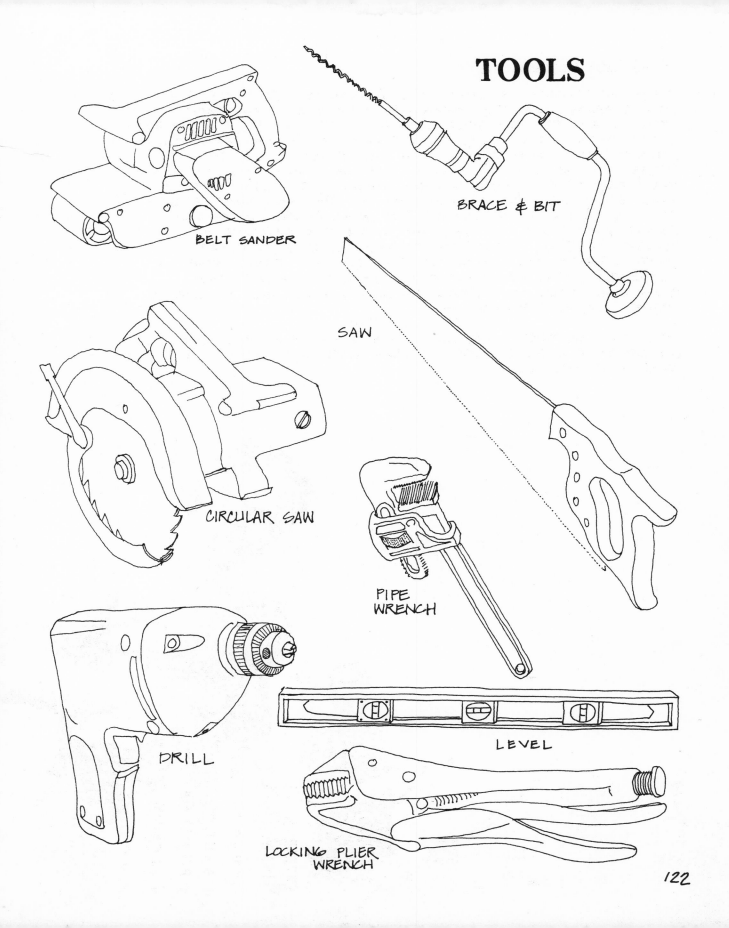

BELT SANDER

BRACE & BIT

SAW

CIRCULAR SAW

PIPE
WRENCH

DRILL

LEVEL

LOCKING PLIER
WRENCH

122

ABOUT THE AUTHOR

M. PAUL FRIEDBERG, DESIGNER AND LANDSCAPE ARCHITECT, HAS WON AWARDS FROM THE AMERICAN SOCIETY OF LANDSCAPE ARCHITECTS, THE NEW YORK COUNCIL OF THE ARTS, THE AMERICAN INSTITUTE OF ARCHITECTS, THE AMERICAN ASSOCIATION OF SCHOOL ADMINISTRATORS AND OTHERS FOR HIS PLAYGROUND DESIGNS, NOTABLY THOSE AT RIIS PLAZA, CARVER PLAZA AND P.S. 166 IN NEW YORK CITY. SOME OF HIS OTHER OUTSTANDING PROJECTS HAVE BEEN THE SPANISH PAVILLION AT THE NEW YORK WORLD'S FAIR, THE U.S. PAVILLION AT THE WORLD'S FAIR IN OSAKA, JAPAN, WATERTOWN EAST AND THE WORCESTER GALLERIA IN MASSACHUSETTS, PEAVEY CONCERT HALL PLAZA IN MINNEAPOLIS, MARTIN LUTHER KING BOULEVARD IN MIAMI, THREE PARKS IN PITTSBURGH, THE FIRST NATIONAL BANK OF DENVER, THE PEDESTRIAN MALL IN MADISON, WISCONSIN, AND THE MOSCOW TRADE CENTER IN RUSSIA.

BORN IN NEW YORK CITY, HE RECEIVED HIS B.S. FROM CORNELL UNIVERSITY AND NOW LIVES IN NEW YORK CITY WITH HIS WIFE AND TWO SONS.